how2become

Achieve 100% Series
Pass Your GCSEs
With Level 9s

www.How2Become.com

As part of this product you have also received FREE access to online tests that will help you to pass your GCSEs.

To gain access, simply go to:

www.MyEducationalTests.co.uk

Get more products for passing any

test at:

www.How2Become.com

Orders: Please contact How2Become Ltd, Suite 14, 50 Churchill Square Business Centre, Kings Hill, Kent ME19 4YU.

You can order through Amazon.co.uk under ISBN 9781911259145, via the website www.How2Become. com or through Gardners.com.

ISBN: 9781911259145

First published in 2017 by How2Become Ltd.

Typeset by How2Become Ltd.

Disclaimer

Every effort has been made to ensure that the information contained within this guide is accurate at the time of publication. How2Become Ltd is not responsible for anyone failing any part of any selection process as a result of the information contained within this guide. How2Become Ltd and their authors cannot accept any responsibility for any errors or omissions within this guide, however caused. No responsibility for loss or damage occasioned by any person acting, or refraining from action, as a result of the material in this publication can be accepted by How2Become Ltd.

The information within this guide does not represent the views of any third party service or organisation.

.

Contents

Introduction

Welcome to our guide to passing your GCSEs with level 9s. In this book, you will learn the essential tips for passing any GCSE subject. From general study tactics to in-depth exam techniques, you will learn exactly what you need to do in order to get the highest marks, and secure the best grade possible.

GCSEs can be tough. They'll test you on a wide range of subjects, and require a lot of work. It's likely that you'll enjoy at least some parts of your GCSE studies, but there will probably be some tedious and gruelling bits too. Hopefully, the advice in this guide will make your GCSEs feel less like an uphill struggle, and more like an enjoyable (and challenging) journey.

What are GCSEs?

General Certificates of Secondary Education (GCSEs) are internationally recognised awards given to students who achieve a pass grade in their exams, coursework and other materials. GCSEs are taken by students in England and Wales, and cover material which is more advanced than the Key Stage 3 (KS3) curriculum, but less intense than A-Level and other higher education qualifications.

GCSEs are available for a broad range of subjects, including the 'core' subjects of English, Maths and Science. Additionally, subjects such as Art, History and Media Studies are available to be studied at GCSE level, although their availability may differ depending on the school. Most students will be familiar with the bulk of these subjects from being taught them at KS3, although there are a few new subjects that are available.

The following subjects are mandatory for all students at GCSE:

- English (Language and Literature)

- Science (Biology, Physics, Chemistry)

- Maths

The following subjects are also available at GCSE. None of these are compulsory, but you must take some of them:

- Art

- Business Studies

- Classics

- Design & Technology

- Drama

- Geography

- Health and Social Care

- History

- ICT

- Latin

- Law

- Media Studies

- Modern Foreign Languages (such as French, Spanish or German)

- Music

- Physical Education

- Politics

- Psychology

- Religious Studies

- Sociology

- Statistics

- Welsh

Usually, schools will allow students to choose from this list of subjects. However, bear in mind that not all subjects will be offered in all schools. Some schools may also require you to study at least one foreign language. Check your own school's GCSE options, to find out more about what you can study at GCSE.

GCSEs are usually awarded to students in year 11 of secondary school. However, in some schools, students may start their GCSE work earlier, in order to finish earlier.

Depending on the subject, the GCSE will be split into different parts. Some subjects, such as Maths and Science, are generally made up entirely of exams, whilst other subjects are made up of coursework and exams. The make-up of each GCSE will also differ depending on the exam board. Some exam boards use coursework more than others. Check which exam board is being used for each of the GCSE subjects in your school, then take a look at each exam board's website, to find out exactly what their GCSE courses comprise of. This way you'll know exactly what to expect from your GCSEs, and can refer to the relevant sections of this book to focus your studies.

To find these details on exam board websites, use a search engine to search for their name. From the main page, you need to navigate either to a 'subjects' page or a 'GCSE' page, depending on the exam board. From there, find your subject and navigate to the specification. You might need to download the specification in order to read it.

Why do they matter?

GCSEs are possibly the most important qualifications you'll earn in your life. When you finally make it into the working world, they'll impact your job prospects, and they are instrumental in the process of accessing higher education such as A-Levels or college courses. In fact, they can even impact your ability to apply for a degree, although this is less common, and A-Level results are generally a bigger factor when applying for university courses.

GCSE results have an indirect effect on further education, because they can have an impact on what A-Levels you can take, and where you can take them. It's for this reason that everyone should take their GCSEs seriously; they set you up for the next qualifications, which will shape the direction of your career.

Aside from this, GCSEs are a great environment to learn about new ideas, letting you figure out which subjects you'd be interested in pursuing further (if any!). Many students choose their A-Level subjects based on enjoyment or performance at GCSE, and some even stick with a subject for degree level or beyond. Therefore, it's worth paying attention in your GCSE lessons, since they may contain interesting material which you will want to pursue in the future.

Finally, GCSEs act as a great environment for learning new revision and studying techniques. They can also act as a 'trial-by-fire' for work ethic, encouraging young people to work harder in order to achieve their goals.

What do I need to pass?

In recent years, the scoring system for GCSEs has moved from using letters (A* being the highest, U being the lowest) to numbers (9 being highest, 1 being lowest, with a U being given in some cases). In the new system, anything higher than a U (i.e. 1-9) is 'technically' a pass.

However, this doesn't mean you should settle for the minimum pass mark. The higher your grade, the better your CV will look; this is vital when applying for higher education and jobs in the future. So, you should aim as high as possible when studying for your GCSEs.

Your school will likely set you a target grade which you should aim to achieve, or exceed if possible. If your school does not set you a grade, look at your results in classwork or mock tests, to choose a target for yourself. Setting high targets will help motivate you, but remember to set goals which are realistic as well. Strike a balance between the two and aim for that grade.

If your school gives you a target grade, and you think that you can achieve higher, aim higher. Don't let yourself be restricted by inaccurate targets if you think that you can exceed them.

Who is this book for?

If you're reading this book, you're probably aiming high in terms of academic achievement. Perhaps you're looking for strategies to use in a particular subject, or perhaps you want more general advice on how to study and how to perform well in exams and coursework. In this book, you will be introduced to general and specific revision techniques which will allow you to unlock your full potential.

Alternatively, you may be completely new to GCSEs, and looking for a head-start to put you in the right direction. This book will help you identify what kind of learner you are, and then give advice on how to make the most out of different learning styles. For instance, you might be a visual learner, in which case you may wish to use videos and mind maps to commit information to memory in a visual way.

It may be the case that you are part-way through your GCSEs and are feeling stressed or nervous about what comes next. This book will give you some techniques and strategies for handling stress, as well as reassuring you that good results can still be salvaged, no matter what point you're at in your studies.

If you're reading this book, you're already demonstrating that you want to go further than the classroom when it comes to your GCSEs. This is great. It shows that you have a strong work ethic, and puts you in an excellent position when it comes to the harder elements of the course.

Finally, you might be a parent reading this on behalf of your child, or perhaps you are reading it in anticipation of your child's future GCSEs. We will include an 'advice for parents' sections where applicable. These will highlight ways in which you can help prepare your child for their GCSEs.

The aim of this book is to provide advice no matter what your situation. If you're reading this because you are sitting GCSEs yourself, or you're reading this on behalf of a family member sitting their GCSEs, then this book will apply to you. Everyone will sit exams, and so the next two chapters are absolutely applicable to your situation. Equally, some students will have to do coursework, and so a chapter is devoted to that as well. The final chapter will focus on a selection of subjects, giving subject-specific information on each.

General Study Techniques

In this chapter, you will be introduced to some general revision techniques, which you can use while preparing for exams or controlled assessments. The three key types of learning – visual, kinaesthetic, aural – will be explained in order to help you identify which way you find most comfortable. By doing this, you will have the opportunity to work *smart*, not just work *hard*. There's not much use in using unsuitable or ineffective learning strategies – find the ones which are compatible with the way in which you think, and use them.

In addition, this chapter will focus on how to use your time effectively when studying. This applies to exam revision, as well as coursework and general classwork. Learning to make use of the resources available to you, and creating a detailed revision timetable, will set you up for success at GCSE level.

Why should I revise?

Revision is the most influential factor in success at most academic levels, including GCSE. Since a lot of GCSE work is based on recalling information, you will need to be able to retain large amounts of knowledge, which you can draw from in your exams.

You might feel that you are naturally intelligent and don't need to revise, or maybe you've been very successful at KS3 and think you can coast through GCSE. Sadly, this isn't the case – you will need to put hard work into your GCSEs in order to get a satisfactory result.

As mentioned in the previous chapter, your GCSEs are the first rung on the qualifications ladder, and it's vital that you get off to a good start. Learning smart revision techniques will help you tremendously if you wish to pursue further education at A-Levels and university especially. GCSEs can be an excellent testing ground for discovering how you work best.

Different types of learning – Visual, Kinaesthetic, Aural

There are three major ways that people revise and absorb information. These are:

- **Visual** – This involves using visual aids such as note-taking and creative mapping of information, to commit things to memory.

- **Aural** – The use of videos, music or other recordings to allow information to sink in.

- **Kinaesthetic** – Using activities which involve interaction, to remember key details (such as flashcards and revision games).

Different paths will work better for different people, but also bear in mind that certain subjects will also suit these methods differently. For example, Maths may be better suited to visual learning than aural learning, because mathematics (sums and equations) is more visually-oriented than other subjects. However, certain rules or formulae could be learned by placing notes around your study space, if you're a kinaesthetic learner.

Essentially, you will need to experiment with different styles in order to find which ones best suit you, but you will also need to discover what works for each of your subjects. In the next three sections, we will examine the different methods of learning in more detail. Additionally, each method will be paired with the subjects which best suit it, as well as how to identify which style matches your own.

The quickest way to figure out what kind of learner you are, is to think of what works best for you when trying to remember something. When someone needs to explain to you how to do something, what sinks in the best? Do you learn by watching others doing it first, or by listening to their explanation? Alternatively, you might learn best by giving it a try yourself. Use the following quick guide to figure out what kind of learner you might be:

- **Visual** – You learn best by watching others or reading information. If you're learning a technique in a game, sport, or other activity, you would prefer to watch videos of others doing it, watching people do it in real-life, or by reading explanations. You might also learn from looking at images or diagrams.

- **Aural** – Listening is your preferred style of learning. You would rather ask for and listen to directions rather than look at a map. If you were learning something new, you'd rather listen to an explanation and follow the instructions.

- **Kinaesthetic** – You learn by doing things rather than just listening or reading. Rather than being told how to do something, you try to do it yourself. You prefer practical, energetic ways of learning as opposed to the traditional methods of reading, listening and note-taking.

Learning Style Quiz

Answer the following 10 questions to figure out what kind of learner you are. Once you're done, head to the answers section where all will be revealed!

1. If you saw the word "dog", written down, how would you react?

A) Imagine a dog in your mind.

B) Say the word "dog" out loud to yourself.

C) Imagine things related to dogs (e.g. barking, playing fetch).

2. You're playing a computer game and you want to figure out how to do something. Which way would you choose?

A) Watch a video of it being done on the internet.

B) Ask someone to explain it to you.

C) Figure it out yourself by attempting to do it.

3. Which of the following would you mostly likely do for fun?

A) Watch a film.

B) Listen to music.

C) Some kind of physical activity.

4. Which way would you prefer to study?

A) Looking at diagrams and images.

B) Listening to a revision podcast.

C) Writing notes on pieces of paper and sticking them on the walls in your room.

5. You've just arrived in a city that you're unfamiliar with. How would you find the local supermarket?

A) Find and follow a map.

B) Ask someone to give you directions.

C) Keep walking around and figure it out for yourself, using landmarks to remember where you are.

6. How would you remember a phone number?

A) Visualise yourself dialling the numbers.

B) Keep saying the phone number out loud.

C) Write it down.

7. When you meet a new person, what do you remember most?

A) Their face.

B) Their name.

C) What you did with them, or what you talked about.

8. Which of these would work best for you while studying?

A) Reading notes.

B) Asking and answering questions with a friend.

C) Taking part in a role-play.

9. You're in a new clothes shop for the first time. Which of the following would you mostly likely remember?

A) The layout of the shop and how it looked.

B) The music that was playing or the sounds that could be heard.

C) The things you liked and tried on.

10. If you heard a song, what would you think of?

A) The music video or the album artwork.

B) The music itself and the lyrics.

C) A memory that you associate with the song.

Now that you've finished, you can find out what kind of learner you are.

If most of your answers were A, then you are a visual learner. You learn by using your eyes to analyse diagrams and notes.

If most of your answers were B, then you are an aural learner. Spoken words sink in best, so you do well when listening to yourself or others.

If most of your answers were C, then you are a kinaesthetic learner. You study best when getting involved and doing things for yourself, rather than watching or listening.

Remember that you don't necessarily have to fall into just one of these three categories. A wide range of learning methods might work for you, so it's good to keep experimenting to find out which techniques suit you best.

In the next few sections, we will cover the three main styles of learning, so you can get some top tips on how to study efficiently!

Visual Learning

Visual learning is exactly as it sounds – you learn by visually representing information, or by having information visually represented for you. This can involve pages of notes, mind maps, tables, animations, slideshows and more. All of these can be used to make information easy to digest visually.

While modern computers are adept at note-taking and mind-map making, you might find it more helpful to ditch the laptop for a while and use a pen and paper. This way, you can improve your handwriting skills, make notes which are available at any time, as well as avoid distractions which come too easily whilst on a computer connected to the internet!

Visual learning is excellent for any subject that has a lot of written text to digest. This applies to everything from English to the sciences, where a passage of information needs to be dissected to find the most important parts. Note-taking can condense a whole chapter of dates, facts and figures into a page or two. Mind maps are a great way of connecting loads of key facts to a single core concept, such as an event or an important person. Additionally, videos and slideshows are excellent for representing data in a clear manner.

Visual learners tend to be good at remembering images and charts. They'll likely find it easier to remember details of pictures and photographs, and might perform well in memory games where they have to spot which object has been removed from a collection. For this reason, visual learners are suited to organising their revision materials into diagrams, which they will likely find easy to remember.

Note-taking and Summarisation

The goal of this method is to collect all of the vital information from your resources. The best way to do this is to underline the key words from sentences in your textbooks or other materials. Once you've done that, you can lay them out in your notes. This is beneficial because it separates the important details from the less important ones. For example:

"Boudicca was a Celtic warrior, queen of the Iceni tribe, who led a resistance against the imperialistic Romans in Britain. At her height, she led an army of approximately 100,000 people."

By underlining all of the key information, we can now organise the facts from the above paragraph into something easier to remember:

Boudicca – Celtic Warrior.

Queen of Iceni Tribe.

Led resistance against Romans in Britain.

Led an army of approx. 100,000.

This method allows you to organise information succinctly, so when you return to read it later, you can absorb the vital facts and leave everything else out. By limiting yourself to these facts, you can focus on the details which are necessary. This is useful because you don't want to overload your brain with long, clunky sentences; when all you need is the important stuff. What's important is that you transfer the notes into an easily digestible format.

For longer pieces of text with more vital information, you may need to write notes in full sentences. This can be a great way to improve your handwriting and writing skills. The other beneficial part of this method comes in the form of re-writing the information in your own words. It may be tempting to fall into the habit of copying information word-for-word, and you might find yourself doing this without even thinking about it. If you're doing this, you're probably not internalising the information, and you might not even understand it properly. There are plenty of machines capable of copying things exactly, but that doesn't mean that they understand the information that they're making copies of! So, you should prove that you understand what you're reading by turning it into your own words. For example:

"Boudicca was a Celtic warrior, queen of the Iceni tribe, who led a resistance against the imperialistic Romans in Britain. At her height, she led an army of approximately 100,000 people."

This could become:

"Boudicca was queen of the Iceni tribe, and a Celtic warrior. She led a rebellion against the Roman army when they invaded Britain. Around 100,000 warriors fought for her while she was at her height."

Here, the content of both texts remains largely the same. However, by writing the work in your own words, you are demonstrating to yourself that you have identified the key parts of the text and understood them. Writing information in your own words is a great way to test your comprehension of the text; if you're able to sum up the message of the paragraph in your own words, then you probably understand its content quite well.

Note: Check with your teacher before underlining or writing in textbooks. If the book doesn't belong to you, it's likely that you won't be allowed to write in it!

Although writing notes allows you to read over them later, the key part of this process is writing them in the first place. When you turn notes from a text into your own writing, you're committing it to memory. Reading it afterwards may be helpful in the short-term, but actually writing it sinks into your head more easily, and it's more likely to become part of your long-term memory.

Visual learners also benefit from making their work more vibrant and striking. This can be done by using different text sizes or colours. For instance, you could write more important words in larger text so that they stand out more. So, when you return to read your notes, you'll see the vital details immediately.

"Boudicca was queen of the Iceni tribe, and a Celtic warrior. She led a rebellion against the Roman army when they invaded Britain. Around 100,000

warriors fought for her while she was at her height."

Different colours could represent different things in your work. For example, if you were given a text including the pros and cons of nuclear energy, you could highlight the positive parts in green and the negative parts in red. Then, you could use a colour such as amber (or orange) to show important details which aren't necessarily positive or negative.

This traffic light system can be used in all sorts of ways. If you were reading a poem for your English Literature GCSE, you might notice different themes. The main (most important) themes could be highlighted in green, less important themes can be highlighted in amber and then the least important themes could be highlighted in red.

You can write up your notes in even more ways. For example, it might be a good idea to split the pros and cons of nuclear power into a table:

Nuclear Power: For or Against?

For	Against
Doesn't produce carbon dioxide (better than fossil fuels). Reduces greenhouse effect, which causes global warming.	Difficult to dispose of.
It's much more efficient than fossil fuels.	Non-renewable (it's going to run out!)
It's a reliable energy source that will last a lot longer than fossil fuel.	Nuclear waste could damage environment.
	Power plants can go into meltdown and cause catastrophe.
	Could lead to stockpiling (hoarding) of uranium, which could be tampered with or stolen by terrorists to create nuclear weapons.
	The UK doesn't have access to a lot of nuclear materials – would have to rely on imports eventually.

Creating tables is a great way to organise information. If you have to, you can make more columns to add other categories. Since the space to write in is usually quite small, you need to be able to summarise ideas briefly in your own words. If you're able to do this, it shows that you understand what the ideas are!

Mind Maps

Another great way of visually representing your notes, is by creating mind maps. These are webs of ideas and information connected to each other, to show how they are related. Generally, a central concept appears in the centre of a page, and then other details spread away from it. This is excellent for quickly jotting down all of the information you can remember, and then organising it into sections.

Videos, Animations and Slideshows

Visual learners can benefit greatly from watching videos and animations to help them revise. There's a wealth of videos online, often made by people who recently sat exams, which can be used to help you get a better grasp of the material. Head over to a popular video-sharing website such as YouTube and search for the topic you're currently revising. Always double-check that the information that they give is correct and relevant (by comparing what the videos say to what's in your own textbooks), because it's possible that these people studied a different curriculum to you.

Outside of the usual video-sharing sites, there are plenty of online resources which will give you videos, animations and slideshows to help you get your head around whatever you're currently revising. Again, remember to check that the information you're receiving matches what's in your textbooks.

This method is great for splitting up long sessions of note-taking. If you've spent the whole day revising, and you're getting tired of writing down notes, watching some revision videos online might provide some relief.

Note: watching videos online can be an excellent way of revising, but make sure that you stay on topic. It's far too easy to get distracted by everything else on the internet (e.g. social media, online games) – stay focused!

Am I a visual learner?

Do you find that you can recall information based on how it's displayed on a page? Try taking some notes or making a mind map based on resources in your textbooks, then turn the paper over and try and re-write the notes. Once you've re-written everything, flip the original page back over and see how well you did at remembering it all. If you were able to remember most or all of it, that probably means that you can learn from visual aids.

Aural Learning

Aural learning is all about listening. Aural learners absorb information by listening to it being said, either by themselves or by others. While it only really involves your ears, aural learning is incredibly flexible. There are plenty of ways to revise effectively if you are an aural learner.

Aural learning is excellent for subjects which have lots of short, sweet bits of information. For example, in your Science GCSE, you might need to remember the process of natural selection. Visual learners will likely write the process down as a series of bullet points, or perhaps a flow chart, whilst aural learners will want to listen to each of these points individually, to allow them to sink in.

Reading out loud

This is the simplest method of aural learning, and can be done on your own and without any extra equipment. All you need is yourself, your textbook (or other study materials) and your voice!

Start by opening on a chapter or paragraph that you're comfortable with, and then begin to read it to yourself out loud. When you come across a sentence or point which might be more complicated or confusing, read it multiple times. By doing this, it will stick in your head more, making you more likely to remember it.

Aural learners can benefit from using certain tones for different points. Singing notes that you need to remember, or creating catchy rhymes for them, can help you to keep them in mind more easily. It might sound silly at first, but they can be incredibly useful.

Aural learners can create acrostics and mnemonics to help them remember difficult spellings or more complex ideas. Acrostics and mnemonics are almost opposites of one another. An acrostic is a phrase you keep in mind to remember lots of smaller phrases or information.

For example, BIDMAS is an acrostic which can be used to remember how you should go about solving maths questions:

Brackets

Indices (or 'powers of')

Division

Multiplication

Addition

Subtraction

Mnemonics, on the other hand, are a collection of words used to remember a single, larger word. These are particularly good for spellings:

BECAUSE = **B**ig **E**lephants **C**an't **A**lways **U**se **S**mall **E**xits

The colours in the rainbow can be remembered using the following mnemonic:

ROYGBIV = **R**ichard **O**f **Y**ork **G**ave **B**attle **I**n **V**ain

You can also use this acrostic to help you remember the colours of the rainbow!

Red

Orange

Yellow

Green

Blue

Indigo

Violet

Aural leaners can repeat the phrase "ROYGBIV" or "Richard of York gave battle in vain" until it sinks in fully. Then, if you got stuck in a test, all you'd need to do is recall the phrase!

Note: any kind of learner can make use of acrostics and mnemonics. Even if you aren't an aural learner, try them yourself!

Self-recording

For this technique, all you need is your voice, some reading material and a device which you can record yourself with. In the past, you would have had to use a specific device called a dictation machine to record yourself. Nowadays, almost any modern smartphone or tablet has voice recording capabilities. So long as it has a microphone, it should be able to record your voice as well. If these options aren't available, dictation machines aren't too expensive, and they might be worth the investment.

Note: Many laptops can record your voice too. If it has a camera, it's probably capable of recording your voice with its microphone!

If you've chosen to use the "reading aloud" method of revision, you might as well record yourself at the same time. The self-recording technique is quite simple; all you need to do is record yourself reading your notes.

The great thing about this method is that both recording and listening help you to remember information. While you're reading your notes out loud into the microphone, you're going to be committing them to memory, just like you would when reading out loud. Once you're done reading all of them, you can listen to them through speakers or headphones whenever you're studying.

Here are some tips to make your recordings even easier to study from:

- Make sure you're not speaking too close to the microphone, or too far away from it. Do a couple of test runs to make sure your microphone is working properly.

- Speak slowly and clearly, so that you can listen back easily.

- Place emphasis on the more important details in your notes. Try changing your tone of voice for certain key phrases or facts, so that they stick out more.

- When you're done recording, send the files to your phone or smart device so that they're always handy.

- Whenever you have a free 10 minutes or so, you can listen to your notes!

Advice for Parents

If possible, make sure that your child has access to a device which can record them speaking. They might need to download additional apps or software in order to do this. If this isn't possible, consider buying them a dictation machine. This could be a great investment, as your child can use it throughout their GCSEs, and for higher education.

Podcasts and other recordings

If you don't like hearing your own voice, or don't have a way to record yourself, there are still plenty of resources that you can listen to. Revision podcasts, such as those on BBC Bitesize, are easily accessible, and quite often free to download and listen to. There are also plenty of resources on YouTube (such as CareerVidz) and other video-sharing websites, which you can listen to via smartphones, computers and tablets.

Remember to make sure that the revision materials are relevant. Depending on the exam board, the topics that you learn may differ. Before listening to a revision podcast, double check that the topics match those in your textbook or syllabus. If you're unsure of where to start, ask your teacher if they know of any resources that may be relevant.

Like self-recording, revision podcasts and other materials are useful because you can carry them with you at any time, with the help of smartphones and tablets. This means that, wherever you are, you can put a bit of time into listening to them.

Another bonus of these techniques is that they can be far less tiring. Reading out loud from a textbook or writing pages upon pages of notes can get incredibly boring, especially after long sessions. Using revision podcasts can often be a slightly more fun way of learning – so make use of it when you aren't feeling entirely up to more formal revision.

Advice for Parents

If you have access to your child's syllabus, find out what exam boards their exams are on. Depending on the board, the topics will differ, and so some resources (such as revision guides and podcasts) won't be as relevant. If you are unsure of the exam boards that your child's exams are on, get in touch with your child's school to find out. Bear in mind that exam boards may differ per subject. So, try and get a list of all your child's subjects and their respective exam boards.

Discussing with others

Many revision techniques can be quite lonely. Sometimes, it's nice to have a bit of human interaction. Thankfully, aural learners can make use of discussion with a revision partner. This is a great revision method if you have a friend or family member available to help. All this involves is sitting (or standing!) with your revision partner and going through the material with them. There are two different ways in which you could do this:

- **Ask and answer questions.** With this method, your revision partner will hold the textbook in front of themselves for them to read, and then ask questions about the material. It's your job to answer them as accurately as possible. If you get the answer correct, congratulations! Move onto the next one. If you answer incorrectly, your revision partner can steer you in the right direction by revealing a bit more information, such as the first letter of the word, or some related details.

If your revision partner is a classmate, then you should try and take turns asking and answering questions. By doing this, you're both being exposed to the material and can get things done quickly.

- **Open discussion.** This method involves you and your revision partner speaking freely about the material. If your partner is also studying for an exam, both of you should try to discuss without looking at your textbooks or notes. However, keep the books close-by in case both of you can't remember something, or are unsure of precise details. It's also a good idea to share notes too, so that you can make sure that you've got something correct.

If your revision partner isn't studying for the exam (such as a family member), allow them to have the book open in front of them, but so that you can't see it. Then, just speak to them about the things that you're revising, and they can fact-check you along the way.

Both of these methods are great ways to learn with a partner, and are an excellent method of making sure that your other revision techniques are working. Discussing with a partner is most beneficial later on during revision, when you've already learned lots of information by yourself, and just want to test your ability to remember it.

Note: Thanks to modern phones and internet, you don't even need to sit in the same room as them in order to revise. There are plenty of communication apps and programs that you can download to your phone, tablet or computer which will let you revise with friends.

Advice for Parents

This is a great opportunity for you to participate in your child's learning. If your child likes the sound of this method, offer to sit down with them and go through some revision material. Start with topics that your child is comfortable with, and use the textbook or their notes to ask questions. If they get the answer correct, let them know, and then move onto the next question. Try and find the key details in the textbook or notes and ask questions about those.

If your child is struggling with a question, try and steer them in the right direction so that they might come to an answer. If they still fail to answer correctly, politely let them know that they got the question wrong. Make sure that you also give them the correct answer, and make a note of where they need to improve. Remember to give them encouragement – you don't want to demoralise them!

Am I an aural learner?

Aural learners tend to focus on what they are hearing and saying more than what they are seeing and doing. If you think this applies to you, give some of the above styles a try. Aural learning is especially useful for those who struggle to sit down and take notes for longer periods of time, and the above techniques can be used by anyone who wants to mix up their revision.

Kinaesthetic Learning

Kinaesthetic learning is all about *doing*, rather than looking or hearing. Kinaesthetic learners shouldn't limit themselves to sitting in one place and trying to write pages full of notes. Instead, they should be finding more creative and unconventional ways of learning. There's a huge range of techniques for a kinaesthetic learner to tap into!

Since kinaesthetic learning is such a broad field, it can apply to almost any subject and any kind of information. If you think you might be a kinaesthetic learner, give some of the following techniques a try.

Flashcards

With flashcards, you'll want to write down some key notes from your textbooks or other revision materials. Take a large piece of card and cut it up into smaller segments. On one side of each card, write down the word or concept that you need to remember the meaning of. On the other, write down the key facts associated with the word. Here's an example to get you started:

Front	Reverse
Sonnet	A fourteen-line poem which is written in iambic pentameter. Uses specific rhyme scheme. Has a single, focused theme.

Once you've written all of your flashcards, turn them all facing front up and sort them into a deck (like a deck of playing cards). Then, take each card, read out the main word on the front, and then try and recall as many of the key facts as possible. You can do this by reading out loud, or by reading in your head – whichever suits you best.

Once you think you've finished listing them all, flip the card over to see if you missed any details. If you didn't, congratulations! Put the card to one side and save it for later. If you missed anything, take note of it and put the card back at the bottom of the deck. This means that, once you've got through all of the other cards, you can attempt the ones you couldn't completely remember before. One by one, you'll start to eliminate cards from the deck, since you'll remember all of the details for each of them. Once you've completed them all, take a short break before trying again.

Another method for using cards is to stick them around your workspace. Write a note on each piece of card and leave it somewhere in your room where you're likely to see it often. Stick some to your mirror or the edge of a laptop screen, or even place them on the wall or on a bookshelf. You can even leave them around your house so that whenever you stop to make yourself a snack or go to the toilet, you'll still be revising!

Advice for Parents

If your child finds placing notes quite effective, it's worth letting them place cards around the house. Let your child place the notes wherever its safe and useful for them to do so.

Multitasking

Multitasking simply involves doing another activity whilst doing your ordinary revision. By doing this, you'll start to associate certain facts with the things you do. If you enjoy exercise, try listening to recordings of yourself reading out notes, while going for a run or working out in some other way. If you play video games, stop and test yourself on a question every so often. This probably won't work as a main revision technique, but it's a way to do some light revision on a day off, or once you've finished the bulk of your studying for the evening.

Learning Games

For this technique, you're probably going to need access to either the internet or dedicated workbooks. You'll want to find games or other interactive tools which involve *doing* things rather than just reading them. For example, one game might require you to match up key words to their meanings, or key dates to the events which occurred on them. You can actually do this one yourself, in the same way that you made flashcards. Cut up a large piece of paper in separate pieces, and then on half of them write a key word. Then write something related to each key word on all of the other pieces. Shuffle up all of the cards, then try to match them up.

You should also check online for other learning games. As always, double check that the content of the games matches what you're learning in class, so you don't confuse yourself.

Am I a kinaesthetic learner?

If you find yourself *doing* things rather than reading or listening, then kinaesthetic learning might be the style for you. You might find that it's much easier for you to do something for yourself, rather than ask someone to explain it to you. You might also find that you work best in unconventional settings: maybe you work better while exercising than sitting at a desk.

A final word about learning styles

The techniques explored here are only a few of the many ways you can learn and revise effectively. Start by experimenting with the methods we've listed, but feel free to branch out and try your own ways of revising. Different people think and work differently to one another, and so you need to find your own unique way of learning that works best for you. Remember that, just because you may believe that you have a specific learning style, you don't have to stick to a limited range of techniques. Be creative and give everything a try – it's the only way to truly know what works best for you.

Revision Timetables and Planning

Now that you've had the opportunity to explore the different ways of learning, it's time to turn the focus to other general aspects of revision: creating and sticking to a timetable, and making full use of revision materials. Both are extremely valuable when revising, and proper handling of both will improve your grade and make you more likely to score high in exams and in controlled assessments.

The goal of having a revision timetable is to map out all of the work that needs to be done in the time after you've started, up until your exams begin. Your plan doesn't need to be expertly crafted or even particularly nice to look at; it just needs to be clear and easy to read.

The first thing you should do is list every subject that you are taking exams in. Once you've done that, try and find every topic or module within that subject.

For example, a breakdown of your History modules may look like this:

Module 1 – History of Medicine

- Diseases and infection: ancient era, renaissance era, industrial era, and modern era;

- Surgery and the human body: ancient surgery, medieval and renaissance surgery, and modern day surgery;

- Public health: pre-industrial era, post-industrial era, and 20th century public health.

Module 2 – Elizabethan England

- Queen Elizabeth and her government;

- Treatment of the poor in Elizabethan England;

- Puritanism;

- Catholicism;

- Shakespeare and theatre in Elizabethan England;

- Naval expansion in Elizabethan England.

You may wish to go into slightly more detail for each of the topics, but as a foundation this will be enough to fill in a revision timetable. Do this for every module and for every subject, so that you know roughly how much material there is to cover. It's also worth taking a look at how long each of the chapters for these modules are in your textbook, so that you're aware of any abnormally large or small topics.

Once you've done this, it's time to prioritise all of your subjects and topics. Some people like to rank all their subjects from most important to least important. In other words, it might be worth considering which subjects you find more difficult, and giving them higher priority. If you already feel quite confident about a certain part of your studies, place it slightly lower on your list. This means that the areas that need the most attention will receive it.

Once you've prioritised your subjects, you can also prioritise modules. Bear in mind that a lot of topics in many subjects are cumulative – which means that a good understanding of earlier modules is vital for getting to grips with later ones. This is especially the case with Maths and Science, where you're building up knowledge as you go along. For these ones, it's better to start at the beginning and work your way through, but other subjects might allow you to mix things up a bit.

Your timetable should include all of the material that you need to revise outside of school hours. The best way to find out what you need to cover, is to take a look at how your textbooks divide their content, and then use those to fill the timetable. You'll be treated to some blank templates for a timetable at the end of this book. The following example timetable shows what a single week of revision during term-time may look like. Take a look at this timetable to get an idea of how to organise your time:

	Monday	Tuesday	Wednesday	Thursday	Friday	Saturday	Sunday
9:00am-10:00am	School	School	School	School	School	English – essay planning	Chemistry – mock paper
10:00am-11:00am	School	School	School	School	School	History – essay planning	Chemistry – mock paper
11:00am-12:00am	School	School	School	School	School	English – mock essay	Physics – mock paper
12:00am-01:00pm	School	School	School	School	School	History – mock essay	Physics – mock paper
01:00pm-02:00pm	School	School	School	School	School	Lunch Break	Lunch Break
02:00pm-03:00pm	School	School	School	School	School	Free Time	Free Time
03:00pm-04:00pm	School	School	School	School	School	Maths – mock paper	Biology – mock paper
04:00pm-05:00pm	Maths – algebra	Physics – electromagnets	Biology – human anatomy	Maths – statistics	History – The Spanish Armada	Maths – mock paper	Biology – mock paper
05:00pm-06:00pm	Maths - trigonometry	Physics – space physics	Biology - homeostasis	English – spelling practice	History – Britain in WW2	Free Time	Free Time
06:00pm-07:00pm	Physics - forces	English – read 19th century novel	Maths – probability	English – reading poetry anthology	English – poetry anthology	Free Time	Free Time
07:00pm-08:00pm	Free Time	Free Time	Free Time	Free Time	Free Time	Free Time	Free Time

Remember to factor in breaks and school time. During term time, you're going to be in school for most of the day, only giving you a couple of hours in the afternoon and evening. Naturally, you're going to feel more tired in the evenings after school than at the weekends, so you might find that doing the bulk of your revision on Saturday and Sunday is helpful.

On the other hand, you might want to do all of your revision during the week, then have relatively little to do at the weekend. Spend the first two weeks of your revision trying out some different routines, find out what works best for you, then stick to one for the duration of the exam season.

During the school holidays, the game changes entirely. All of a sudden you don't have to go to school for 6 hours a day, meaning that you have a lot more time on your hands. While you may want to take a break from everything, you should make use of all the free time you have during these breaks. In fact, many students do the bulk of their revision during these holidays. Of course, you should take some time off, but make sure you take advantage of the holiday period. This can really put you ahead for the next term.

How do I motivate myself?

Getting motivated to revise in the first place can be incredibly difficult, and requires a lot of determination and self-control. The earlier you start your revision, the better, but you'll probably be tempted to put off revision: "I'll start next week", or "it's way too early to start revising."

Try and start revising 8 weeks before your first exam. This should give you plenty of time to get through all of your topics.

However, even starting the process can be a pain, and when the exams are so far away it's difficult to get the ball rolling. So, you need to motivate yourself to start revising as early and as well as possible. Here are some ways to inspire yourself to start revising:

Revision Styles

Start by finding revision styles that you actually enjoy. This might sound ridiculous, but if you can find a few techniques that aren't completely unbearable, you'll be more willing to make a start with revision. Remember that you don't have to be constantly doing 'hard revision' such as note-taking. Mix things up and try a number of styles to keep things fresh early on, then maybe move into something more serious later.

Ease into it

Before you start, revision can feel like a huge mountain, impossible to climb to the top of. It can be incredibly daunting. You might be overwhelmed by the feeling that you are completely unprepared and don't know enough. That said, you need to make a start sometime. Some revision is better than no revision at all, so if you're struggling to get started with your studies, ease your way into it. Start by revising for a much shorter period of time, and maybe focus on the things that you already know well or most enjoy. Once you're comfortable and confident, move onto something that you're less sure of.

Treat Yourself

Make sure you keep yourself motivated with some treats. You don't need to go overboard, but the "carrot and stick" method of revision can keep you working for longer periods of time, allowing you to get through more work. Things like "I'll get some ice cream, but only after I've done the next 3 pages" are a great way of keeping you going and keeping your spirits up.

Think Ahead

Finally, always think ahead past exams. Life continues after your GCSEs, and you'll be treated to an extra-long summer once you've finished. You might feel that you're not in a great place while revising, that your social life is suffering or your free time is being eaten up by studies, but it will all be worth it when you get great results. This positive outlook – thinking towards the future – is one of the best ways to get you started with revision, and keep you going with it too.

Staying Focused

Sometimes, revision can be a total pain, and you'd rather do anything (even sit around doing absolutely nothing!) than open a book and do some hard learning. It's very tempting to procrastinate, but falling into the trap of putting off revision is one of the biggest mistakes you can possibly do.

Here are our top 5 tips for avoiding procrastination and getting on with your work!

1. Turn off distractions

The first thing you should do before starting a revision session is remove any distractions from your workspace. The biggest offenders for distracting pupils are games consoles, social media, mobile phones, and of course television. The simple solution to this is to turn off these devices, and put them somewhere out of view or reach, so you aren't tempted to turn them back on and continue texting, messaging or playing games.

Sometimes, however, it isn't practical to move all of these devices. In this case, it's better to find a new workspace, free of electronic devices and other distractions. Many people find that their kitchen or dining room table is an excellent place to study, but find what works best for you and your home. If there's nowhere in your house that's suitable for studying, the local library may be a good choice.

- When choosing a place to study, consider the following:

- Is it quiet?

- Are there any gadgets to distract you?

- Will people be walking in and out of the room? Will that distract you?

- Is it comfortable?

- Is there plenty of room for you and all of your notes?

Things get a little trickier when you're using computerised or other online resources such as revision games or podcasts. In these cases, you're going to need your computer, phone or tablet with you, so you'll need to exercise some self-control. Log yourself out of social media if you feel that it's necessary to do so, and make sure to turn off notifications for messaging apps on your phone. You can always take a look during your breaks.

Finally, a few words about listening to music while revising. Be very careful when playing music (especially music with lyrics) while studying. It works for some people, but others will find it incredibly distracting. Experiment with it for yourself, but if you find that it doesn't help you, promptly turn it off.

Advice for Parents

If possible, make sure that your child has a dedicated space to revise in. Preferably, this place should be far away from any kind of distraction, including noise caused by family. Try to keep the noise down while your child is revising, but occasionally popping in to show support can make a world of difference.

---

2. Give yourself plenty of breaks (but not too many!)

Believe it or not, one of the best ways to avoid procrastination is to take regular breaks. Concentration tends to slide after 45 minutes for a lot of teenagers, so don't push yourself to revise for longer periods of time. If you do this, you'll likely get distracted by almost everything around you, or just get bored or tired. The solution to this problem is to place regular breaks after every chunk of time spent revising. So, if you revise for 45 minutes, you should give yourself a 10 or 15-minute break afterwards. Start with this and then adjust it as necessary, until you get into a routine which is comfortable for you. Remember not to go overboard with breaks. Make sure that you stick to your timetable and routine, so that a 15-minute break doesn't turn into an hour spent watching TV!

3. Stick to your revision timetable

Writing and filling in a revision timetable is one thing, but it's another thing entirely to stick to it throughout your entire exam season. If it helps, make your timetable more detailed to include breaks and other activities.

It can be tempting to put off revision or bargain with yourself: "I'll only do 2 hours today but I'll make up for it tomorrow," or "I don't really need to know this stuff, I'll take the rest of the day off." Both of these are risky mind-sets, which don't put you in a great place for succeeding. Good organisation skills come in handy here, and you should try and keep to your timetable as much as possible.

Of course, you can be flexible with your time. Sometimes things come up, and you shouldn't completely sacrifice your social life during the revision period. Just make sure it's reasonable, though.

4. Make your working environment comfortable

Outside of keeping things quiet and free from distracting gadgets, you should make sure that your revision space is comfortable enough for you to work in. If the room is too cold or hot, or your chair isn't comfortable to sit on, then you might find yourself not wanting to revise. Make sure your revision space is as comfortable as possible.

Advice for Parents

Ask your child if they like their revision space. If they don't, find out what the problem is and try to help them solve it.

---

5. Mix things up

The final tip for staying focused is to mix things up every so often. One way to do this, is to change the subject that you're revising halfway through the day. This means that you'll still be revising, and you'll keep things fresh. You don't need to switch it up too often, but when you find yourself getting too bored of a topic to continue, finish it and then move onto something else entirely, preferably an area from another subject.

You could also change your revision techniques from time to time, to keep things interesting. If you've spent the whole morning writing notes, why not switch over to a podcast or some learning games? You can refer back to our section on different learning styles to get some ideas on how to make your revision more varied.

Avoid Cramming!

Cramming is the act of trying to stuff in as much revision as possible in the days (or even hours!) just before the exam. It's also possibly the biggest act of sabotage that you can do to yourself.

Cramming happens when a pupil either does very little or no revision before the exams. Before they know it, the exam dates have crept up on them, sending them into a state of panic. These pupils tend to then rush through their textbooks and materials, trying to cover weeks' worth of work in just a few days. In almost every case, this is simply not enough time to adequately revise everything. So, people who cram very rarely benefit from it.

Cramming can actually worsen your performance in an exam. Students who cram often find themselves completely blanking on information when they start answering questions, leaving them helpless during an exam. Cramming doesn't work because you aren't giving your brain enough time to let information sink in.

In an ideal world, you should try to finish your revision for a subject 2 or 3 days before the exam starts. This doesn't always go to plan, but aim to have your revision finished at least 2 days before. Revising the night before an exam is a bad idea, and you should avoid doing so. The day before your exam (and in the hours leading up to it as well) should be spent relaxing and keeping calm, eating well and not allowing yourself to become stressed out by looming thoughts about the test. If you get to the day before your exam and you've finished everything, then you've done an excellent job, and deserve an evening to relax.

Advice for Parents

Keep an eye on your child's revision schedule, and every so often check that they're on top of their work. You don't want to intrude too much, but a subtle reminder might make sure that your child doesn't let their exams creep up on them.

Conclusion

So, by this point you hopefully have the following: a revision timetable, a comfortable space to work, an idea of what your learning style is, and some ideas to get you started with revision. You're now well on your way to taking your GCSEs and succeeding.

Next, we'll be looking at exams: what they are, how to deal with revising for them, and how to perform well in them!

Exam
Techniques and
Preparation

What are exams?

By now, hopefully you'll have your exam timetable ready, with some learning and revision techniques to get you on your way.

At some point during your GCSEs, you're going to come across at least one exam. This is pretty much unavoidable, because every subject at GCSE uses examinations to assess your knowledge, understanding and ability. Exams can be incredibly daunting, but in this chapter you'll learn what they are and how to deal with them effectively.

An exam is a type of test that you take in a controlled environment. In most cases, exams test your knowledge and understanding. You will need to remember information that you've learned for the subject throughout your GCSE years. Sometimes you'll just need to recall facts, but in other cases you'll have to apply your understanding and knowledge to a situation. This could involve essay writing (such as in English or History), or problem solving (such as in Maths).

This means that you have to sit in silence, for at least 45 minutes (and often longer), and finish a paper full of questions. The length of the exam will differ depending on the subject, module, and even exam board. If you are unsure about the length of any of your exams, speak to your teacher or check the relevant exam board websites.

Exam conditions are incredibly strict. Once you enter the exam hall, you can't speak to anyone. You are strictly limited to the time given to the exam, and if you're caught cheating in any way, you can be disqualified from all of your exams.

Thankfully, it isn't all doom and gloom. Exams are tough, but they aren't designed to be impossible or even cruel. If you prepare effectively using the tips and techniques in this book, and revise lots, you'll be more than ready to take on your exams.

Advice for Parents

If your child is unsure about what exams they are sitting, give them a hand by finding out what exam boards they are on. Once you've done this, head to the exam board's site(s) to find out details on the exams that your child is going to sit.

Types of Exam

There are a number of different kinds of exam you might sit. Here are some of the most common kinds:

- **Essay exams.** These exams require you to write longer pieces of work rather than answer lots of small questions. These will be most common in English literature and English language.

- **Short-question exams.** These exams will have lots of questions, each being worth a smaller amount of marks than a full question in an essay exam. Marks usually vary in length, depending on how much the question is asking from you. Single-word answers are usually only worth one mark, whilst a longer Maths question might be worth 3, 5 or even 10 marks. Short exam questions will show up across a range of subjects.

- **Hybrid exams.** These exams will feature longer and shorter questions, as well as some essay questions. History and Science exams often have slightly longer essays, as well as some shorter questions at GCSE.

As well as this, there are some further general exams that you might have to sit:

- **Listening exams.** This is most common in Modern Foreign Languages. You'll have a recording played to you, and you will need to answer questions in a booklet based on what you are hearing.

- **Speaking exams.** Again, these are quite common when studying a foreign language. Unlike your other exams, speaking exams usually won't require you to enter an exam hall with lots of other students. Instead, you'll sit one-to-one with a member of staff, and will have to speak to them in the language you are studying. They will ask questions, and you'll have to answer back in the same language.

The Tiers: Foundation and Higher

Currently, GCSEs are split into two tiers – foundation and higher. Depending on your ability, you will be entered into your GCSEs at one of these two levels. There are a few differences between the two tiers that you need to know about, since they affect what type of exam you will sit.

Firstly, the content of a course may differ depending on whether you're on the foundation or higher tier. Some subjects are quite similar in structure between the two tiers, but may offer different content. For example, a foundation-tier Maths course may contain the same format and kind of questions as a higher-tier course, but students in the higher-tier will be expected to have a better understanding of maths, and also be able to complete more demanding questions.

In other subjects, the mark scheme will be different depending on the tier students sit. For example, a foundation-tier English paper might ask students to describe a scene from a book that they've studied, whilst a higher-tier exam may ask for analysis or evaluation as well. For this reason, it's important to know what tier you're being entered for before starting revision, attempting mock papers or reading mark schemes.

As we've established, higher-tier papers are generally more demanding than foundation-tier exams. They'll either contain trickier content, expect a higher level of analysis or discussion, or have a different structure. Quite often, a higher-tier exam will consist of all three of these differences.

So, why take a higher-tier course if it's generally harder? The benefit of sitting a higher-tier paper is that you will be able to get a higher grade. Students on a foundation-tier course can get a grade between 1 and 5, whilst the grading for higher-tier courses ranges from the middle of a level 3 up to a level 9.

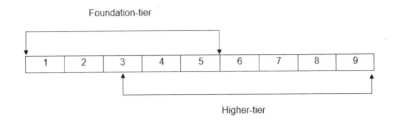

Foundation-tier

Higher-tier

It's in your best interest to find out what tier you're going to be in. Remember that tiers can differ between subjects, so don't assume you're in one tier for every one of your GCSEs. Ask your teachers what tier you're going to be entered for, so that you know what to prepare for in the exams.

Exam Tips and Techniques

Exams can be difficult, and you need to prepare for them in two different ways. First, you need to know the content of the exam. This is the actual information that you are going to be tested on – the stuff you've been learning in lessons.

The second thing you need to learn is how to answer exam questions, and how to perform well in exams. This might sound strange, but a significant part of doing well in exams comes down to your familiarity with them, not just how well you know your subjects.

In a later chapter, we'll discuss subject-specific tips for exams. For now, take a look at these general tips, which will help you in the days before and during your exams.

Come Prepared

Always make sure that you have all of the equipment necessary for completing an exam. This will depend on the subject and the module, so find out beforehand what you're allowed to take in with you.

The following are things that you can take into almost any exam:

- **Black pens.** You should always take a few black ballpoint pens into your exams. Generally speaking, blue pens are not allowed, neither are fountain-pens, since the ink can run more easily on them. Ballpoints are the standard for most exam boards.

- **Pencils.** You might not need these for every exam, but it's worth bringing them for rough planning, just in case.

- **Clear pencil case.** Again, this might not be necessary, but bringing a pencil case can help you be more organised. Make sure it's clear though – if the exam invigilators can't see into the pencil case easily, they may confiscate it because you could be using it to hide notes and cheat!

- **Bottle of water.** We'll talk more about this later on, but bringing a bottle of water can help you concentrate – you don't want to get dehydrated. Remember to make sure that the bottle is clear and has no labels.

Depending on the exam, other pieces of equipment may be appropriate, such as:

- **Calculator.** Certain Maths and Science exams will allow you to bring calculators. Other exams in these subjects might not allow for calculators. If you aren't sure, bring it with you anyway and then leave it under your desk, and hand it to an invigilator if it isn't allowed.

- **Rulers and protractors.** Equipment for solving angles may be allowed for some exams. Like calculators, however, they won't be allowed for others. Make sure that they are transparent (clear).

- **Books.** Be careful with this one. Some exams might allow you to bring in a specific book, such as some English or language exams. Others will be referred to as 'closed-book' exams, which means you can't take in any notes or materials – including the books that you've studied.

If you aren't sure which equipment you're allowed to bring into the exam, ask your teacher well in advance.

Keep Calm

Getting a handle on your nerves can be really difficult during exam season, but remember that this is completely normal. If you consider that doing well in your GCSEs is very important, then it would be bizarre for you not to be at least a bit nervous. Millions of people will be going through the same thing as you, and millions more have been in your position and have made it out of the other end in one piece. Life goes on after your GCSEs, even if it doesn't feel like that during the heat of an exam.

Exams are stressful, and the conditions you take them in aren't pleasant either. Being stuck in a silent room for an hour, with nothing but a question paper and your own thoughts, can be incredibly daunting. However, you need to remember that you're not the only one who feels this way, and that a bit of nerves can give you the boost you need in the exam hall.

That said, you need to keep any anxiety under control. A breakdown just before the exam (or even worse, during it) is uncommon, but just remember that not doing as well as you'd hoped in a single exam isn't the end of the world.

You might feel as though you aren't prepared enough, or perhaps a classmate has made you unsure about what you've revised – minutes before entering the exam room. This happens often, and be incredibly demoralising. Remember that how prepared you think you are doesn't necessarily represent how well prepared you actually are. Sometimes, people who feel poorly prepared for some exams in the minutes before taking it end up doing incredibly well, and some people find themselves doing worse in exams that they felt completely ready for. Essentially, you never truly know how prepared you are.

Besides, what's the use in worrying on the day of the exam? There's no time left to go back and revise some more, so there's no point in getting stressed about it once you're in the room. Try and get into the current moment and power through it.

Here are some other tips for keeping calm in the exam:

- **Breathing exercises.** If you find yourself getting nervous before exams, or struggle to get to sleep due to exam anxiety, then breathing exercises could be beneficial.

- **Get into the moment.** Just before and during your exam, it can help to go into "exam-mode". By this, we mean blocking off outside distractions and any negativity coming from anywhere. Sometimes, having friends and classmates talk about the possible contents of the exam just before entering can put you off. It might make you feel as if you've missed out on something major, and then cause you to worry once you enter the exam room. Put all of this out of your mind as soon as you enter the room. Once you're in the exam, there's no use fretting about those details.

- **Positive thinking**. This might seem obvious, but thinking positively about the exam and what comes after can be extremely helpful. Some people like to change their mind-set about exams, thinking of it as an opportunity to show off their knowledge, rather than as a painful task that they have to work their way through. Alternatively, focus on what you **do** know rather than what you **don't** know, what you **can** do rather than what you **can't** do. Once you're in the exam room, there's no point worrying about your weaknesses. Focus on your strengths.

Read Instructions Carefully

This sounds simple, but far too many people trip up on

this simple bit of advice. When you enter your exam, the first thing you should do is read the instructions on the front of the question or answer paper. In some cases, an invigilator may read the instructions to you, but feel free to read the instructions before the exam starts.

Keep an eye out for instructions on what questions to answer. In some exams, you'll have a choice of which questions you answer, rather than having to answer every question. In these cases, you need to make sure that you know exactly what's required of you, so that you don't waste time answering questions that you don't need to answer. The only thing worse than finding out at the end of the exam that you answered questions unnecessarily, is realising that you didn't answer enough of them!

When you are given a choice of two or more questions to answer (especially in essay subjects), make sure you clearly show which questions you are answering. In some exams, you'll have to tick a box to show what question you're attempting, whilst others will require you to write the question number in your answer section. Either way, keep an eye on the instructions before going ahead and starting the question. This will prevent you from wasting time answering questions that you don't need to attempt, and also stop you from accidentally missing questions that need answering.

When it comes to some questions, more things may be required from you than just giving a single answer. In a lot of Maths exams, you will be asked to show your working. By this, it's simply meant that you must show

how you got to your answer if you want to get more marks. Sometimes, minimal marks are given if you don't show your working, so it's vital that you include how you made your way to the answer. Keep an eye out for questions which specify that you must "show your working" – you'll need to make sure that you do it to get as many marks as possible. By showing your working out, means that you may pick up a couple of marks, even if you get the answer wrong!

Answer the Easiest Questions First

This tip is absolutely key for the tougher exams you come across, since it's an excellent way to use your time in the exam hall effectively.

Say you're about to sit an exam. You sit down and have the examination instructions read out to you. The invigilator instructs you to start your exam, and then you begin. You open the question booklet to find that the first question seems almost impossible. Before you panic, take a flick through the booklet and take a look at some of the other questions. If possible, pick the question that looks the easiest to you and start with that.

This is a good technique for two reasons. Firstly, it's a great boost to your confidence when you're feeling unsure about the exam. There's not much worse in an exam than sitting there, becoming more and more demoralised by a question that you don't think you can answer. Starting with more manageable questions will help you ease into the exam, and hopefully you'll recall some information while doing it.

Sometimes, exams can fit together like a puzzle. At first, it seems impossible. But, once you start to put pieces in (answer the questions), the more difficult bits start to make sense. All of a sudden, you're on a roll of answering questions, and then the tough ones don't seem so bad!

The other reason that this is a good technique, is that it represents a good use of your time. There's no point sitting and staring blankly at a question that you can't solve, when there are others that you could be getting on with. Forget about the tough questions for now, bank as many marks you can get with the easier ones, then go back to the hard ones at the end if you have time. This way, you can secure as many marks as possible. In the worst case scenario, you won't be able to complete the tough questions, but you'll still have earned a few points for all of the others.

Answer the Question

One of the biggest mistakes that students make throughout their academic lives is failing to answer the question that they've actually been asked. This is particularly the case for essay-based exams such as English Literature, but applies to all of your exams.

Focus on Key Details

Some students have a tendency to read a question briefly, then jump straight into their answer without thinking about what's really being asked. For questions which are worth lots of marks, you should take extra care in reading the question fully. If it helps, underline the key parts of the question, so that it's easier to break down:

What were the main causes of the First World War?

This becomes:

What were the <u>main causes</u> of the <u>First World War</u>?

We can figure out a few things from underlining the key points in this question. Firstly, we know that the topic of the question is the First World War. In particular, we need to be looking at the causes of the war. So, our answer is going to be focused on the time period leading up to the start of the First World War in 1914.

However, there's more to the question than this. This question specifies the "main" causes of the First World War. So, we don't need to talk about every single cause of the war, just a few of the most important or biggest things which caused the First World War to happen, such as the assassination of Archduke Franz Ferdinand and rising tensions between the European empires.

<u>Already, we've figured out that we need to answer the question in the following way:</u>

- You need to talk about the causes of the First World War (events up to 1914).

- You need to limit your answer to the main (biggest) causes of the war.

Highlighting the key points of the question has proven useful, because it's pointed out exactly what the question is asking of us. This means that we can save time by answering exactly what we need to, rather than talking about things that won't get us any extra marks.

Don't Twist the Question

Sometimes, students see a question that they don't particularly like the look of. Perhaps it's for a topic that they've studied well and enjoyed, but the question takes a slightly different direction to one that they're used to. For example, a student may have studied the Shakespeare play *Othello* as part of English Literature, and really liked the dastardly villain, Iago. In the exam, they might come across a question on the play, but not specifically about Iago. The question could be:

How does Shakespeare show the relationship between Othello and his wife, Desdemona?

This question is primarily focused on the main character, Othello, and his wife, Desdemona. While the character of Iago plays into most elements of *Othello*, it might be tricky to include him in a discussion about the relationship between Othello and Desdemona. So, you'd need to avoid straying from the topic of the question, even if there's something you would rather write about. Twisting the question into something that you want to answer is a trap that quite a lot of students fall into, and this ends up costing them marks – particularly in essay subjects. Writing a short plan for your answer, and reading the question carefully, can help you avoid this.

Double-Check the Question

In the next section, we'll be talking about double-checking answers, but it's just as important to double-check the question that you're answering, before you begin to answer it. Say you're doing a maths question:

$$8.93 \times 9.54 = ?$$

Before you start answering the question, take note of everything about it. Where are the decimal points? What operation needs to be performed? Sometimes, people make silly mistakes and misread the question, getting things mixed up.

It's not pleasant finding out that you've answered a question incorrectly just as you get to the end of it, so it pays to look over the question multiple times. In the case of maths questions, it might help to re-write the question in the answer box if there's space. This means you can look back at it quickly, without making any mistakes.

Don't Hedge Your Bets

Hedging your bets happens when a student tries to give 2 or more answers to a single question, trying to cover as many bases as possible and be less likely to lose marks. After all, if you give lots of different answers, surely one of them is bound to be correct? The problem with this is that examiners will mark harshly against answers like these. Take a look at this example of someone who has tried to hedge their bets:

Question: What part of the human body carries blood back to the heart?

Answer: Veins/Arteries

Only one of the given answers can be correct, since one of them sends blood away from the heart and the other brings blood back to it. The correct answer is "veins", but in this example, both possible answers have been put in. This example answer shows that whoever answered the question wasn't sure, so put both down just in case. Examiners will not award marks for this, so it's essential that you don't try to play it safe in this way. Be confident in your answer.

Avoid Blanking

Have you ever been in a situation where you had something in your head that you were about to say, or about to write, but then completely forgot what it was just before saying or writing it? It can be frustrating in everyday life, but when it happens in an exam it can lead to all kinds of problems. Key details can be forgotten, formulas and tricks may be hard to recall, and sometimes you might just struggle to get off the first page. This is what people refer to as 'blanking'.

Blanking is something that many students worry about, and you've likely heard some horror stories about people who have forgotten everything just as they enter the exam room. However, it doesn't occur as often as you might think, and it doesn't mean you're going to fail your exam.

The best way to prevent blanking is to keep stress to a minimum. This might be easier said than done, but students tend to blank when they haven't had much sleep or have tried to cram their revision into the day before, or the day of the exam itself. This can cause students to panic, and while they're busy worrying, anything that might have been holding in their short-term memory gets forgotten. We'll cover stress in more detail later in this chapter.

In addition to keeping stress to a minimum, make sure that you aren't revising on the day of your exam, and preferably not the night before, either. In order to retain the information in your revision, you need to commit it to what some people call your 'long-term memory'. It takes time for what you've studied to reach this part of your memory, and things revised in the hours before the exam usually haven't made it there. When revision is being held in the short-term memory, you're generally more likely to forget it, which in turn leads to blanking.

If you find that you've blanked in your exam, here are some tips to keep you calm and help you recover from it as quickly as possible:

Take a few deep breaths before continuing. This is important as you need to stay calm. The more you panic, the less likely you are to remember the information you need. Take a moment to calm down – remember that not performing so well on this exam isn't the end of the world, and that you have the entire paper to remember what you need to know and get back on form.

Look through the question booklet. Sometimes, the

wording of a question can jog your memory, or give you a clue of what to write. This can get you started on an answer, which in turn can set off a chain-reaction of memories flooding back, to the point where you remember plenty of information. However, this doesn't always happen; don't rely on this as a replacement for revising over a longer period of time.

Start with an easier question. Some questions require less knowledge than others. If you find yourself blanking in the exam, go onto a question that doesn't need as much precise information as others. Sometimes, a question won't be asking for specific terms or details, but rather an analysis or critical take on the material. These are the questions to do first if you find yourself blanking. This won't work for every kind of exam, however.

Don't attempt any of the larger questions. It might be tempting to just throw caution to the wind and get the toughest or biggest question out of the way. This is usually a bad idea, since these questions contain the most marks. You want to answer these once you've remembered as much as possible, so wait until later in the exam to try them.

It's not the end of the world. If you find yourself running out of time, don't panic. Answer as many questions as you can to secure as many marks as possible. It isn't the end of the world if you don't do so well, and you'll have other exams in which to pick up some marks.

Double-Check Your Work

Everyone makes mistakes. It's almost completely

unavoidable, even under relaxed conditions, to create a piece of work that's free of any errors at all. In an exam, you're going to feel a bit rushed, and you're probably going to be working very quickly. This is fine, but remember that you're more likely to make mistakes this way. So, it's important that you go back and check everything you've written. Small, silly errors can cost you big marks, so it's vital to make sure you've fixed anything that could be wrong.

Proofreading can take place at two times during your exam. You can either re-read each of your answers individually after you've completed each one, or you can go back at the end of the exam (if you have time) and check every question in one go. There are benefits and drawbacks to both:

Proofread as you go

Pros	Cons
You're more likely to have time to double-check your answers.	If you spend too long proofreading, you might not finish the exam.
You can take the exam bit by bit.	You might be in "exam-mode" and not be as relaxed as at the end of the exam.

Proofread at the end

Pros	Cons
You can focus on finishing the exam first before going back to check.	If you take too long doing the exam, you might not have time to proofread towards the end.
You'll probably be more relaxed once you've answered all the questions.	

Both have pros and cons, and one method may just suit you better. You might prefer the methodical approach of checking every answer once you've finished it. Alternatively, you might find it easier to handle the exam, knowing that you've answered every question that you can, and then go back and check everything in one go.

How to go about proofreading your work will depend on the subject that you're taking, and the questions that you've been asked. If you've had to write essays or other longer bits of text, read over your work, checking for errors. Re-read the question, and make sure that you've answered properly. If you haven't done this, quickly add the extra information in the answer box.

If you've missed something out of an essay, the best thing to do is put a little asterisk symbol (*) where you'd like to add more information. Then, in the next available space (possible even at the end of the essay), put another asterisk, followed by the information that you've missed out on.

When you double-check your work, you might come across something that you've written, but that you know now is incorrect. In this case, you need to cross it out, so that the person marking your exam knows to ignore these incorrect parts. Put a straight, diagonal line through your work, to indicate any work that you don't want the examiner to look at. Then, all you need to do is replace what you've crossed out with something that's correct.

Bring Some Water and Eat Healthily

You are allowed to bring a bottle of water into almost any exam. There may be a couple of exceptions for practical-based exams – such as Art, but aside from that, water is allowed. In fact, bringing a bottle of water to drink in an exam is largely encouraged, because it can help you relax and concentrate.

Some studies show that students who take a bottle of water into their exams and drink it get an average score of 5% higher than students who do not. While this might not actually happen for you, this suggests that having a bottle of water handy can be helpful.

On the same topic, eating healthily (and sensibly!) before your exams can make a big difference. Try and avoid drinking fizzy drinks or eating sweets before an exam. The sugar rush might make you feel on top of the world when the exam starts, but you could have a crash halfway through, leaving you shattered for the final stretch. Instead, try and have a good breakfast in the morning before your exams. See what works best for you, but eggs and fish (such as smoked salmon) can give you plenty of energy to complete your exams with.

In addition to this, some exams may allow you to bring in a small piece of food to eat. Fruit is always a safe bet, including bananas and apples. Basically, you want something that doesn't take too long to eat, but gives you enough of a boost to help you through the exam. Remember to check that you're allowed to take food into your exam before doing so.

Stay Healthy

No matter what happens in your exams, it's important that you stay healthy. This is a slightly more general point, but it can't be emphasised enough.

First, you need to stay mentally healthy. Remember that there's life after your exams, and so you shouldn't put yourself under unnecessary pressure. Some anxiety is unavoidable, but it's important that you don't let it get out of control. Between exams, remember to do things that you enjoy, be it sports, video-games, reading fiction, watching television or spending time with friends or family. This will help you to feel calm during your exam period, and remind you that there's more to life than your GCSEs!

Secondly, you need to think about your physical wellbeing. While you're busy revising and making yourself ready to ace the exams, it's easy to forget about your own health. While it's good to take revision seriously, you can't neglect your own physical needs, and so you should make sure to get a lot of the following during your exam period:

- **Sleep.** Everyone needs sleep in order to function, and you're no different! Teenagers need between 8 and 10 hours of sleep per night, so you should be aiming for this as well. A good night's sleep, particularly the night before your exam, can make a world of difference on the day of the test. It will also help you massively during your revision time.

- **A balanced diet.** This can be easily overlooked, but being fed well can be the key to acing an exam on the day. You want to feel as prepared as possible, so be sure to get a good meal the night before and on the day of your exam. Also try to eat plenty of fruit and vegetables, since they help strengthen your immune system. Some students work themselves extremely hard, then forget to boost their immunity, leading to colds and flu. You want to avoid this – being ill during an exam is horrible!

Planning and Timing Your Exam

Good planning and timing are two of the most important skills that you can learn and practise before sitting your exams. In fact, being able to plan effectively and get your timing down will serve you well in almost every career, so it pays to put the effort in now.

Before you go into your exam, you should find out exactly what the structure of the exam will be. Try and find out the answers to the following questions:

- How long do I have for the whole exam?

- What type of questions will be asked (essay,

single-word answer, short paragraph, problem solving, mathematical sums)?

- How many marks are there in the whole exam?

- Roughly, how many marks are available per question?

- If applicable, how much time is there for planning?

Once you have this information, you can get to work on applying this to your revision schedule. For example, when you attempt a mock exam, you should try to make the situation as close to the real thing as possible. You should plan and time your mock exam as if it were an actual exam. You can find more about planning and timing your exams in the chapter on subject-specific advice.

Using Mock Exams

Once you're well into your revision, you'll find that you've got lots of information swimming around in your head. When you feel like you're getting to this point, it may be time to attempt a mock exam. These are excellent ways of testing how much you already know, and it also gives you an insight into what you still need to do in order to ace your exams.

Mock exams are so useful that some people use them and no other techniques when revising. This isn't strictly advised – it's better that you start by revising your notes before trying a mock test, mainly because you may not know enough or remember enough to fully complete a mock exam.

How do I find mock exams?

Finding mock exams is usually quite easy. The first port of call is your school or your teacher. It's possible that they have some mock exams already printed to give to you. If they don't, then it might be worth suggesting that they make some available for yourself and other students.

If your teacher doesn't have any mock exams prepared, try and find out as much about the exam(s) you want to revise for before looking up papers. The easiest resources to access are past papers, or actual exams from previous years. These are free to download from exam board websites and can be read from your computer screen, or printed off so that you can write on them.

In addition, there are plenty of workbooks specific to your subjects which will include practice papers and sample questions. You can find out about our range of GCSE workbooks at the end of this book, or navigate to www.how2become.com/school-education.

Advice for Parents

Printing pages upon pages of past papers can get expensive, but it can be a vital way for your child to learn where their strengths lie and where they need to improve. A solution which will allow your child to take advantage of mock papers, as well as save you money on printer ink, is to find settings on your printer such as 'draft' or 'ink saver' mode. These will print the past papers out in a slightly lower quality, but usually the papers are still entirely useable.

How should I use mock exams?

There are two different ways to use mock exams in your revision. The first way is to attempt a full mock essay as you work through topics of the subject. For example, say that you have a Science exam with three different sections. One of these sections is on evolution and adaptation, the next is on the human anatomy, and the final section is about how drugs and other substances can have an effect on the body. You figure out that these are the three topics you need to learn, so you go through past papers online, focusing on questions revolving around these three topics.

Alternatively, you can work through every topic for the exam, and then move onto past papers. The advantage of this method means that you can spend a chunk of time focusing completely on taking notes and using other revision techniques, then move onto working through whole mock papers. This means that you can simulate the experience of being in an actual exam.

Simulating exam conditions

Mock papers and past papers are really useful because they allow you to sit a test as if it was the real thing. To do this, find out how much time you would be given to finish the paper in an actual exam – this information can usually be found on the front of the past paper. Then, gather your pens, pencils and other tools, put your notes aside and find a quiet place. Then, get to work with the mock test.

Time yourself with a clock or stopwatch (most mobile phones come equipped with a stopwatch), and see how long it takes you to complete the paper. What's even more useful is to time how long each section, or even each question, takes you to complete. So, if you find yourself running short on time, you know exactly which topics or types of question need greater focus. You don't want to try and speed through your paper too quickly, but if you're taking an unusually long amount of time on shorter questions, then you know that you need to improve on them.

The best part of using mock exams and past papers is that you can put yourself to the test, and make sure of two things. Firstly, you can make sure that you can recall the material you'll need to remember in the real exam. This comes into effect when you simulate a real exam environment, by doing the test under timed conditions and without your notes. While you're doing the mock tests, you'll probably get an idea of what you can and can't recall. Whenever you can't remember the answer to a question, or there's a key fact you can't recall, make a note on a spare sheet of paper, or at the side of your answer booklet. Then, once you finish the paper, you know exactly what you need to go back to and revise some more.

Mock tests are also useful because they highlight things that you thought you knew, but perhaps didn't get entirely correct. This will become clear when you take a look at the mark scheme, which we will cover in more detail later on in this chapter.

After the past papers...

Once you're finished with the mock paper, look at the mark scheme and see how well you did. For subjects with clear "right or wrong" answers, such as Maths or Science, this is quite easy – all you need to do is read the answer then see if it matches what you wrote. For essay-based subjects such as English, this is trickier since the answers you give aren't necessarily right or wrong. In these exams, you tend to be judged on how well you write rather than what you write exactly. In this case, you might need help from your teacher.

Ask your teacher to take a look at your past papers, and they might be able to take a quick look at it. If they have the time, they might go ahead and mark it properly, giving you an idea of where you've done well and where you need to improve. If possible, get a full breakdown of marks so you know exactly what aspects of your exam you need to focus on.

In the next section, we'll examine a mark scheme in more detail. You'll learn how they work, and more importantly how to use them to make your revision more focused. For now, feast your eyes on the flowcharts. These show two different ways of including mock tests in your revision strategy.

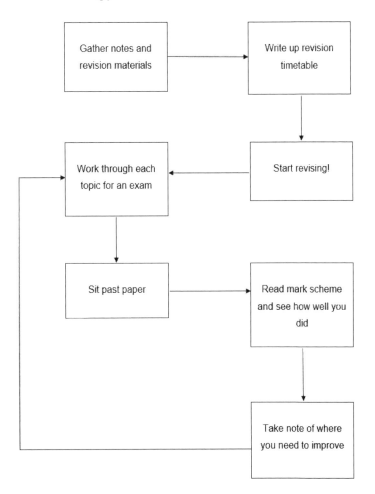

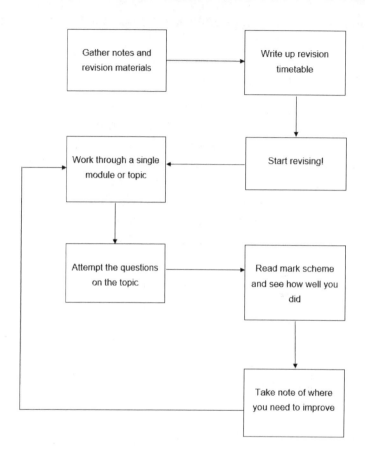

Mark Schemes

Once you've done some practice papers, you'll want to know how well you've done. As we've mentioned previously, mock papers show you what you need to remember, what you know and what you need to improve on. However, sitting the paper is only half of the story.

You'll also need to use a mark scheme to figure out what you do and don't know.

What are mark schemes?

Mark schemes are papers which examiners use when marking your exam. In the case of past papers, the mark schemes are the same ones which official GCSE examiners would use to mark your exams. So, they're the most accurate source for answers. Depending on the exam, a mark scheme will include different content. For example, Science exams will often simply give the correct answers since the questions are either right or wrong.

However, answers to essays in English papers aren't as straightforward. For exams with plenty of essay questions, the examiner will have criteria that they will need to look for in order to figure out what the quality of your work is. This is reflected in the mark scheme with a detailed description of what a higher level essay will look like, and will compare it to other essays of all quality levels. This can make it difficult to mark your own essays, so having your teacher mark them is very useful.

Mark schemes and answer sections can usually be found in the same place where you downloaded the practice papers. Keep away from looking at the mark schemes until you've finished the papers – you don't want to spoil the tests – but have them ready to go.

Why should I use a mark scheme?

Exam Criteria – Essays

Mark schemes have uses beyond simply finding out whether you have the answers right or wrong. In fact, reading mark schemes can be useful even if you aren't sitting a past paper because they'll show you what type of answers that the examiners are looking for. This is especially the case in essay-based exams, such as English, as well as other exams which include essays, such as Modern Foreign Languages, History and Geography. You can use mark schemes to find out what criteria the examiners use to mark your exams, and then compare what you've written to see how well you've done. Have you mentioned the key information that's listed for each answer? Have you answered the questions clearly, using an appropriate structure? Have you checked your spelling? All of these are going to be picked up on in essay-based exams, but it's worth reading a mark scheme to see how much each of these aspects affect your grade.

Jumping Through Hoops and Keywords

The other useful aspect of mark schemes is that they'll reveal key phrases and terms, that will automatically improve your grade if you include them. This is an example of GCSEs requiring you to "jump through hoops" in order to succeed. Even in the subjects where there are no true right or wrong answers, there are often vital ingredients which you need to make reference to in order to secure marks. For example, a science question may look like this:

> *How do animals change their traits over time?*

This question is clearly about evolution. You could answer it like this:

> *Animals are born with some small mutations in their genes. If these animals with the mutation are able to breed, new traits such as larger ears or better camouflage on their fur may start to appear over time. If these traits are advantageous, the animals with these traits will continue to reproduce and pass on their genes, whilst those without the genes will struggle to survive. Eventually, this means that all those without the genes will have died out, and those with the trait will be all that's left.*

This is an adequate explanation for everyday use. However, in the exam you might be expected to give the name of this process as well. Since there have been multiple theories of evolution throughout history, the examiners will be expecting you to show that you know this is called "natural selection" – the theory of evolution discovered and developed by Charles Darwin, which is accepted today.

Sometimes, a mark scheme will specify that certain words or phrases need to be included in the answer in order to get the maximum number of marks. In some cases, these words need to be included to get any marks at all. For the above answer, you would be better off answering it with the following:

Animals are born with some small mutations in their genes. If these animals with the mutation are able to breed, new traits such as larger ears or better camouflage on their fur may start to appear over time. If these traits are advantageous, the animals with these traits will continue to reproduce and pass on their genes, whilst those without the genes will struggle to survive. Eventually, this means that all those without the genes will have died out, and those with the trait will be all that's left. <u>This process is known as natural selection.</u>

Adding this at the end of your answer makes it more likely that you'll secure more marks. Mark schemes are helpful here because reading them will reveal what kind of key words the examiners are looking for. Look through a few years' worth of mark schemes to see if there are any patterns. Are there any words or phrases which pop up a lot? If so, then these are ones that are certainly worth remembering in case you need to call on them in the exam.

It can be incredibly frustrating to know what something is, and be able to describe it (like in the answer above) but not remember the exact name of it. To get around this problem, it's a good idea to use flashcards in revision – they help you associate key phrases with their meanings and examples.

Exact Breakdown of Marks

Mark schemes can also be used to get an exact breakdown of an answer. Using the same example, the answer may award a single mark for lots of different things. For this question, let's pretend that this answer is worth 4 marks.

Animals are born with some small mutations in their genes. If these animals with the mutation are able to breed, new traits such as larger ears or better camouflage on their fur may start to appear over time. If these traits are advantageous, the animals with these traits will continue to reproduce and pass on their genes, whilst those without the genes will struggle to survive. Eventually, this means that all those without the genes will have died out, and those with the trait will be all that's left. This process is known as natural selection.

The mark scheme could award marks for the following:

- 1 mark for mentioning mutations in genes.

- 1 mark for discussing traits.

- 1 mark for including advantageous/disadvantageous traits.

- 1 mark for giving the name of the process – natural selection.

Animals are born with some small mutations in their genes. If these animals with the mutation are able to breed, new traits such as larger ears or better camouflage on their fur may start to appear over time. If these traits are advantageous, the animals with these traits will continue to reproduce and pass on their genes, whilst those without the genes will struggle to survive. Eventually, this means that all those without the genes will have died out, and those with the trait will be all that's left. This process is known as natural selection.

So, the breakdown of marks tells you exactly what you need to include in your answer, which will give you an idea of what you need to remember for the exam. Bear in mind that you might need to know more than what's given in the mark schemes, since you could be faced with a question which tackles the same topic but from a slightly different angle.

This information in the mark scheme means you could focus your answer even more. You might notice that a lot of the example answer is not underlined, and these details might not be necessary in order to gain full marks. With the information in the mark scheme, we can simplify and focus our answer:

> *Animals are born with some small mutations in their genes. If these animals breed, new traits such as larger ears or better camouflage on their fur may start to appear over time. If these traits are advantageous, the animals with these traits will continue to reproduce and pass on their genes, whilst those without the genes will struggle to survive. This process is known as natural selection.*

So, we now have a much shorter answer, which will give us as many marks as the longer answer would. This saves time, allowing us to move onto other questions in the exam.

Giving Precise Answers

In an exam, you might be tempted to fire off everything

you know about a topic all at once. While it's great that you've remembered lots of information, it's not always a good idea to write absolutely everything you know when answering a question. Instead, you should figure out exactly what the question is asking from you. In the above example, we included a lot of information that wasn't necessary to get full marks.

You should aim to be as precise as possible with your answer – get straight to the point in order to save time. Mark schemes are useful here, because they'll show you what the examiners are looking for. You can figure out what's required to get full marks in a question, then focus on giving that as your answer. In an exam, every second is precious; the less time you spend on unnecessary information, the more time you have for harder questions or for double-checking your work at the end. Efficiency is a great skill to have when it comes to exams, and using mark schemes to hone your answers will help you to achieve this.

As well as saving you time, working on giving precise answers can make you sound more confident when giving your answers. Too much information can come across as waffle. While this isn't so much of an issue at GCSE, it's good to get into the habit of avoiding waffle if you want to go on to A-Levels.

With all this said, it's important that you make sure you answer every question in an exam as fully as possible. If you aren't sure what to write in your answer, it's better to give more information than less.

Stress

What is stress?

Stress is an unpleasant sensation that you feel when you're under too much pressure. It's a common feeling to have as a student, especially when studying for and sitting your GCSE exams. The pressure that you feel can sometimes grow to become too much to deal with, and can be bad for your physical and mental health, as well as your GCSE performance.

Stress can be the result of several different worries about your GCSEs. Worries can include:

- Will I get the grades I want/need?

- Have I revised enough?

- Have I left it too late to start revising?

- What will my family and friends think of me if I don't do well?

- What if bad questions show up in my exam?

- What if I oversleep and miss my exam?

- What if I get into the exam hall and forget everything?

Rest assured that, no matter what you're worried about in the run-up to your exams, thousands of other students have felt similar things. It's quite normal to feel a bit stressed during the exam period. However, it's important to keep these pressures in check, and prevent stress from harming you or your chances of acing your GCSEs.

The rest of this section will be devoted to discussing stress, and will hopefully give you some advice on how to manage and prevent it.

How do I know if I'm feeling exam stress?

It can be difficult to know if you're stressed or not. Some people are genuinely stressed, but dismiss it as normal – perhaps because they do not know any different. If you're feeling stressed at all, it's important to identify it and make steps against it before stress becomes too much to handle.

The symptoms of stress occur because, when the body is under pressure, it releases hormones which trigger 'fight or flight' responses in the body. In prehistoric times, these symptoms may have proven useful for preparing the body to protect itself from a threat, or be able to run away quickly. Nowadays, we aren't particularly worried about fighting or escaping from wild animals, so the symptoms of stress aren't particularly helpful.

Stress has both emotional and physical symptoms. If you have any of the following symptoms, and feel unable to cope, then you might be stressed:

Emotional Symptoms	Physical Symptoms
Low self-esteem	Trouble sleeping
Anxiety	Sweating
Constant worrying	Loss of appetite
Short temper	Loss of concentration
	Headaches
	Dizziness

Whether you think you feel these symptoms or not, keep reading to find some methods for preventing stress, and some ways to reduce the stress that you may already have.

How can I prevent exam stress?

First of all, remember that exam stress is completely normal for students sitting their GCSEs. Your GCSEs are very important, and if you're feeling stressed about them it at least shows that you recognise their significance. While stress definitely isn't a good thing, the bright side of it is that you and your body are aware of how important your GCSEs are. Now what's needed is to keep your stress levels down so you can operate at peak performance, and more importantly stay healthy in body and mind!

This section will cover the "dos" and "don'ts" for dealing with exam stress, both during revision and the exams themselves.

DO…

Start revision early. This might seem obvious by now, but starting your revision earlier in the year is one of the best ways to avoid stress. The more time you have, the less you need to do each day. This gives you more free time, and also allows you to make use of extra time to do other revision activities such as practice papers.

Have a countdown to the end of your exams. Buy a calendar and make note of all your exam dates. Tick days off as they go by, and stay focused on the end. Staying aware of the end point of your exams will remind you that there's life after your GCSEs. There is light at the end of the tunnel.

Listen to your body. At times, you might feel like an unstoppable machine, speeding through revision. During this period, it can be tempting to ignore your bodily needs and soldier on. Likewise, when you're worried about not finishing your revision in time for the exam, it seems like a good idea to stay up all night to make up lost time. Whether you're ignoring your body because you're doing well or poorly, it isn't advisable to do so. You can't function properly without food, water and sleep, so remember to take the breaks in your revision to do these things. That way, when you come back to revising, your study sessions will be more valuable because you're able to focus harder.

Forget about the exam once it's over. It's likely that you'll have more than one exam. You might even have multiple exams on consecutive days, or even on the same day. So, it's important not to linger on an exam once you've finished it. As soon as the exam ends, you have permission to forget about it entirely. Try to avoid talking to others about details of the exam, because it might give you second thoughts about what you wrote in yours. There's no use worrying now since there's no way of changing what you've written. Stay confident and move onto the next exam.

Remember that exams aren't the be-all and end-all. As we've already mentioned, life won't end if you don't get top marks in an exam. You might be disappointed by your grade, but remember that life goes on and your exam results won't ruin your life. What's just as important is a confident and prepared attitude, so even if you don't do as well as you'd hoped to, you should focus on moving forward, learning from your mistakes, and enjoying life.

Ask others for support. No person is an island, and everyone occasionally needs someone else to help them through tough times. Exams can be difficult, and a lot of pressure is put on students taking their GCSEs. When the going gets tough, don't be afraid to talk to your friends and family. Find people you trust and talk to them about your worries. Sometimes, just talking about things can make you feel calmer, even if you don't figure out any solutions. More often than not, your worries will be amplified by the general worry of exams, and so talking through your problems and rationalising them can be a form of therapy. You might find that your worries are just the result of paranoia, and aren't grounded in reality.

DON'T...

Rely on online forums. The internet can be an excellent place to find information and techniques for studying. You have access to plenty of specific advice on a range of subjects, and this can supplement your work in the classroom and your revision at home. However, not all resources are useful, and not all environments on the internet are good for your wellbeing. Some exam-focused chatrooms and forums can do more harm than good. You may come across people who are arrogant about the work that they've done, trying to make you feel worse about your studies as a result. Make use of the internet when it comes to your GCSEs, but try not to linger in places that won't make you feel better about your own studies.

Pay attention to how much revision others are doing. You'll likely find classmates who are all too willing to let you know how much revision they're doing, and how well their revision is going. These people are probably having a really hard time with their revision, and are just looking for a way to feel better about themselves. If you need to, ignore these people until your exams are over, and instead spend your free time with people who don't stress you out as much.

Get lazy because your friend has done less revision than you. Just as you'll probably come across someone who's apparently done a lot of revision, you probably have a friend or classmate who has apparently done no revision at all, or very little. While they might be telling the truth, it's also possible that they've actually done quite a lot of revision and they claim to have done little in order to look cool. It's tempting to get lazy about your revision because there's someone else who's done less, but remember that exams aren't about how well others are doing: it's about how well **you** are doing. In turn, this could lead to stress as you realise that you haven't done enough just before the exam. Make sure that you avoid getting lazy with your revision, and this will be far less likely to happen.

Set goals you can't meet. Always remember that there's only so much that you can do each day when it comes to revision. If you've put together a revision timetable then this shouldn't be a problem, but double-check how much work you've allotted for each day. During the revision period, take note of how much you're doing each day, and adjust your timetable based on this. For example, if you're finding that 10 topics is far too many, try reducing it to 7 or 8. Likewise, if you're able to do loads more than 5, experiment and see how many topics you get through in one day. The aim of this is to finish each day satisfied that you did everything you can, and that everything is completed. This should work towards preventing exam stress.

Panic about your exam timetable. Occasionally, you might not meet all of your goals for the day. While this isn't a good thing, you need to remember that you always have the next day to cover what you failed to achieve the day before. At the end of your revision for the day, you should try and put yourself in the mind-set that everything is fine – meaning that you can relax and get some quality sleep.

Rely on caffeine or other stimulants. Caffeine will affect your concentration and sleep-patterns. If you become dependent on it, you'll find yourself unable to perform properly without it, which could lead to uncomfortable and unproductive revision sessions. This could cause stress over time, as you require a certain chemical in your body in order to feel ready to study or sit an exam. In addition, interrupting your sleeping-pattern can make you feel tired during your study time, and can cause stress in general. Do yourself a favour and keep away from the caffeine during the exam period.

Advice for Parents

Stress is felt amongst most students sitting their GCSEs. While it's normal to be slightly anxious about exams, you should keep an eye on how your child is behaving. As a teenager, your child may be quite defensive or quiet about their feelings towards exams, but if you see any of the symptoms listed earlier in this section, you should consider helping them. Here are a few of the ways in which you can help your child avoid feeling stressed during their exam period:

- **Make sure that they know you're happy to talk with them about their worries.** You don't need to pester your child, but if you notice that they're stressed, reminding them that they can talk to you whenever might convince them to open up a bit and talk. This could help them relieve lots of built-up stress.

- **Set time aside to talk to them if necessary.** Don't just let your child know that you're there to talk to, make sure that you're available at relatively short notice. This might not be possible during your own working hours, but while you're not at work, be ready to stop what you're doing and chat with your child. They'll really appreciate you being able to talk whenever they need you.

- **Respect their free time.** Teenagers hate being nagged to do things, especially revision. You need to make sure that they're actually working, but you also need to respect their free time and not interrupt them. One way to fix this is to ask for a copy of your child's revision timetable, so that you know when they should be working and when they will be taking a break. This means that you know not to disrupt their breaks or free time by asking them whether they should be working or not. Your child will appreciate this, since it allows them to relax after a hard day of revision.

- **Give your child what they need to succeed.** Make sure your child has good food, to help them study and prevent stress. Ask them if there's anything in particular that they feel is necessary in order for them to do well, and help them in any way you can.

Conclusion

In many ways, exams are incredibly cruel, and can be very harsh. Just remember that almost everyone that you know has done GCSE exams before you, and people know what you are going through. In this chapter, you've been given lots of tips for coping with revision, as well as how to make sure that you are operating at peak performance during the exam itself.

However, if there's absolutely one thing that you must take away from this, it's that exams aren't the be-all and end-all in your life. They're certainly important, and you should take them seriously, but don't let yourself become distraught over worries about exams, or results which weren't as high as you might have hoped. There's much more to life than your GCSEs.

In the next chapter, we'll be discussing the ins and outs of coursework.

Coursework
and Controlled
Assessment

What is Coursework?

Coursework is a form of assessment which takes place outside of an examination room. Generally, it's a longer piece of work which is completed over a series of weeks or even months. Coursework can involve research or development of an idea, and tends to be more common in essay-based subjects, as well as technology subjects such as ICT.

Sometimes, coursework appears as a piece of work completed over a long period. In other cases, coursework is more controlled. In these circumstances, students usually research and take notes over a few weeks or months, then write up their work in a controlled, exam-style environment. Students are limited to what notes they can bring with them. In recent years, this method of controlled assessment has become more common than the less restricted model.

Until 2016, coursework was a common method of study at GCSE level, but this has been changing over the past few years. Now, only a few of the mainstream GCSE subjects contain coursework, and even these are being phased out in the near future. This means that, if you are reading this book and will be sitting your GCSE exams in 2018 or later, a lot of this chapter will not apply to you. If you're in doubt about whether your subjects include coursework, go onto the relevant exam board websites and look at the specification for your subjects. In particular, take a look at what year the syllabus is changing (if at all). You'll find details about the entire assessment scheme, including exams and coursework.

If coursework does not appear on the specification page, then it's likely that you don't have to do any.

Since coursework has been phased out of most GCSE subjects, it isn't likely you'll have to do much of it. However, in this chapter you'll get some tips for completing coursework on-time and to an excellent standard.

Start as soon as possible

Many students make the mistake of putting coursework off because they think the deadline is far off in the distance. You might not need to write up the final piece until months away, so why bother doing any work now? This is an easy trap to fall into, but must be avoided to perform well. Find out from your teacher as soon as possible what the topic of your coursework is, and what suitable work you can do. In some cases, this might be reading or research, whilst in other scenarios it could be simply becoming familiar with the material. Whatever the case, try to get started as soon as you can – it'll pay off as you approach the deadline.

Get a structure and stick to it

When your coursework takes place over weeks or months, it's easy for it to get out of control and lose any sense of coherence. What you end up with when you reach the deadline might be completely different to what you intended it to be. This isn't always a bad thing, but having a plan for your coursework as soon as possible is a good idea, because it means you have more control over what you're making.

<u>There are two different things to consider when starting a piece of coursework:</u>

• How to plan your time;

• How to plan your work.

Getting together a plan of how you're going to use your time when completing your coursework is key to making sure you meet the deadline with everything finished. You don't need to keep a completely strict schedule, but having structure will keep you working and stop coursework from piling up. In this example, let's say that you have a controlled assessment in History. You know that you'll have to write all your work in a few sittings and in a controlled environment, essentially under exam conditions. However, up until that point you'll need to be doing research, taking notes, planning your essays and possibly writing up drafts, just so you can get an idea of what you're going to write in the real thing.

Since most controlled assessments are completed earlier in the year (before the revision starts), you're able to devote plenty of time to your coursework. Here's an example plan over 8 weeks, leading up to the deadline. For each week, there are a few objectives to meet, followed by some other considerations relevant to the task.

Week Number	Objective
Week 1	Decide on question(s) or topic(s) (if there's a choice): • Which questions seem most interesting? Start a mind map of ideas, considering the following: • What is the question asking? • What general areas do I need to research?
Week 2	Begin research on the topic: • What sources are available? • Do I need to find additional sources? • How many sources do I need to include? Construct a timeline of events which relates to the topic you're writing about.
Week 3	Start making notes based on research. Remember to include where you got your ideas from. Try to get a mixture of statistics and other facts.

Week 4	Construct a rough essay plan: • What's the word limit for the controlled assessment? • How many points do I need to cover? • What is the argument I want to make?
Week 5	Make your plan more detailed by applying the notes you've made to your rough plan: • Try and have plenty of evidence for each point you're going to make. • Make note of which evidence you've already used for a point so that you don't re-use the same content. • Write a rough conclusion for your essays, so that you have a good idea what the end point of your work is.
Week 6	Try writing some of your points as full sentences rather than rough notes, then have a go at linking your points together in full paragraphs.
Week 7	Try writing a full essay based on your plan. You can use this to get some practice in typing up a piece of work in a short space of time.
Week 8	Final week – write the coursework in a controlled environment.

This is a rough plan for a single subject. Of course, the type of work you'll be doing will depend on what the subject is, and therefore what's appropriate in a plan will change. However, the table above should give you an idea of how to complete an extended piece of work before jumping into it.

Remember that some subjects prevent you from taking coursework home, in order to prevent students from cheating or tampering with their own work. Consult your teacher before taking any work home. If your teacher has constructed a week-by-week plan, try making use of theirs before creating your own.

Make use of multiple drafts

If you are doing a long-term piece of coursework that allows for the teacher to read and mark your work, make use of it. Some students will simply work on their draft, finish it and then forget about their coursework until the deadline, when they hand in the exact same piece of work. Multiple drafts are there to help you refine your work, so make use of them as much as possible.

Listen to feedback

If you get the opportunity to have your drafts read by a teacher, listen and take on board what they suggest you improve on. Sometimes it can be difficult to look at criticism of your work, but it's essential if you want to make your coursework better. Bear in mind that your teacher is there to help you, not attack your work or embarrass you.

Don't try and finish it in one sitting

Some students try to complete all of their coursework in one go – usually the night before the deadline. This is never a good idea, and often results in rushed work full of errors. Earlier in this chapter, we provided an example week-by-week plan of how to bring a piece of coursework to completion. Create one of these for yourself and follow it to make sure that you aren't suddenly faced with a mountain of work the night before the deadline.

Proofread

Proofreading has been talked about in the exam techniques section, but it's just as important when completing coursework. Double check everything you've written or made. If possible, compare it to a mark scheme, to ensure that you have met all of the requirements to get the grade that you want.

Depending on what kind of coursework you're doing, you're going to want to look out for different things. Of course, checking spelling, punctuation and grammar is important for any piece of work, but you also need to make sure that the content is sound as well. If you've included statistics or other facts in your work, go and compare what you've written to the place you found the information. Do the numbers all add up? Are the facts correct? Make sure that what you've presented is as accurate as possible before submission.

Avoid plagiarism

Plagiarism is the act of reproducing somebody else's work without their permission, and is taken very seriously by both schools and exam boards – especially when it comes to coursework. It isn't so much of a concern in exams, since copying someone else's work is difficult and doesn't happen often, but in coursework there are lots of regulations to make sure that students hand in work that is their own. This could be one of the reasons why coursework has moved from a less-restricted, open task, to something more structured and controlled, with students finishing their controlled assessment in a classroom while being supervised.

Whatever the case, avoiding plagiarism is vital when completing coursework. Not only is it against regulations and can result in your work being disqualified, but it's also unfair on the people who have worked hard to create the material that you might be copying. Whether it's your classmate, a website, or a book, you should never copy someone else's work.

Conclusion

As previously mentioned, coursework is becoming less relevant every year, and it's entirely possible that you haven't had to complete any at all, depending on your subject choices. If you do have coursework, think of it less as an obstacle or a chore, and more of an opportunity to score marks before entering your exams. The better you do in your coursework, the more secure your overall grade will be if the exams don't go quite as well as planned.

In the next chapter, we'll cover the core GCSE subjects, along with subject-specific advice on how to revise for them and ace the exam.

Subject-Specific
Revision Advice

So far, you've learned loads of general information about acing your GCSEs. In this chapter, the focus will be shifted onto specific revision and study tips for different subjects. The 'core' subjects of English, Maths, and Science are covered here, as well as handful of other popular subjects taken at GCSE level. We will discuss the general format of their exams, some key advice on how to prepare for them, as well as what you should expect from coursework and exams for each subject. The subjects which will be discussed are:

- Maths;

- English – Literature and Language;

- Science;

- Modern Foreign Languages;

- History;

- Geography.

Maths – Revision and Exam

From 2017 onwards, GCSE Maths involves taking 3 exams. They are all worth 33% of your total GCSE Maths grade, and are all sat at the end of your GCSE course, which will be in June of year 11.

Each exam is 90 minutes long. The first paper is a non-calculator paper, so this section will focus on questions which you can solve without using a calculator, or questions that for which a calculator isn't relevant. The second and third papers are calculator exams, so you are allowed to use a calculator (and will probably need it for at least some questions).

The difficulty of questions in these papers increases as you progress through it. Generally, the simplest questions will be at the start of the paper, whilst the most demanding will appear at the end. Some questions will be worth one mark, and others will require multiple steps to find the answer. The longer questions will be worth more marks, however.

The topics which are covered in GCSE Maths are:

- Number;

- Algebra;

- Ratio, proportion and rates of change;

- Geometry and measures;

- Probability;

- Statistics.

Calculators

Across many subjects, some exams will allow the use of calculators. Before continuing, it's important to note what kind of calculators are allowed in the exam. Essentially, the rules are designed to prevent students from bringing calculators with information stored on them into the exam. Stationery shops will let you know which calculators are exam-friendly, and which are not.

If you already own a calculator, but you aren't sure if

it will be allowed in the exam, ask your teacher well in advance, so that you have time to buy a replacement if necessary.

Tips for Maths Revision

Many students find that Maths is one of their toughest subjects at school. So, if you feel that you're having a hard time with this subject, don't worry – you're not alone. Thankfully, revising for mathematics is generally quite straightforward; all you need to do is practise. You can split revision for into two sections:

Learn the techniques. This is the part of revision where you go over the key techniques and methods for solving maths questions. In particular, you want to find ways of committing these techniques to memory. For example, BIDMAS is a way of remembering the order which you should do mathematical functions in:

Brackets

Indices

Division

Multiplication

Addition

Subtraction

BIDMAS makes it easy to remember this order. There are other techniques you may need to learn, such as the rules for trigonometry:

$$Sin = \frac{Opposite}{Hypotenuse} \quad \text{(SOH)}$$

$$Cos = \frac{Adjacent}{Hypotenuse} \quad \text{(CAH)}$$

$$Tan = \frac{Opposite}{Adjacent} \quad \text{(TOA)}$$

When put together, this reads as "SOHCAHTOA", which can be turned into a saying:

Some **O**ld **H**ag **C**racked **A**ll **H**er **T**eeth **O**n **A**pples.

You can find a lot of acronyms and mnemonics online, or you can come up with your own. Practise with each until you can remember them easily.

Practise the techniques. Once you can recall all of the techniques easily, it's time to put them to the test. Find some practice papers and get to work. Earlier in this book, we discussed how to get hold of practice questions. Start with any textbooks you've been supplied with by your teacher. Generally, those will contain sample questions for each major technique or operation that you'll have to make use of in your exams. Once you've used those, you'll want to move on to other workbooks and online resources.

Remember to make use of mark schemes to make sure you're getting the answers right. If you get the answer wrong, try it again. If you're still struggling to answer the question after a few attempts, refer to any textbooks to see if your methodology is incorrect. Try and go through the question with your textbook or notes to help you.

In the exam...

At GCSE, you will have three Maths exams. Each of these exams is 1 hour and 30 minutes long, and the total mark for each paper is 80. So, this means that you have just over 1 minute for each mark (1.125 minutes, or 1 minute, 7 seconds to be exact). You can use this general rule to figure out how much time you should spend on each question. So, for an 8-mark question, you should give yourself about 8 minutes, 55 seconds to complete it. This means you can keep yourself on schedule to complete the paper.

As always, feel free to answer the easiest questions first. Usually, the less demanding questions appear at the start of the paper, but it might be the case that you find some techniques or types of question easier than others. Read through the whole paper at least once before you start, and then begin by answering the question you find easiest. Work your way up from there.

Alternatively, you might want to go for some of the more demanding questions while your memory is fresh. This works for some students, but only attempt this tactic if you're confident that it'll benefit you. There's no shame in starting with the simpler questions and securing yourself some easy marks.

Write down any rules or techniques that you've remembered as soon as the exam begins, such as SOHCAHTOA, BIDMAS, and so on. This means you don't need to worry about remembering them while you're answering questions, giving you the time and energy to focus on scoring marks.

English – Revision and Exam

At GCSE, English is divided into two separate subjects – English Literature and English Language. Depending on your exam board, these questions may be worth between 40% and 60% of your overall English Literature or English Language GCSE:

	AQA	Edexcel
English Literature paper 1	1 hour, 45 minutes 64 marks Worth 40% of English Literature GCSE	1 hour, 45 minutes 80 marks Worth 50% of English Literature GCSE
English Literature paper 2	2 hours, 15 minutes 96 marks Worth 60% of English Literature GCSE	2 hours, 15 minutes 80 marks Worth 50% of English Literature GCSE
English Language paper 1	1 hour, 45 minutes 80 marks Worth 50% of English Language GCSE	1 hour, 45 minutes 64 marks Worth 40% of English Language GCSE
English Language paper 2	1 hour, 45 minutes 80 marks Worth 50% of English Language GCSE	2 hours 96 marks Worth 60% of English Language GCSE

As you can see, marks are weighted slightly differently, depending on which exam board your course is on.

Find out from your teacher about what exam board your English course is on, before planning your revision.

The final thing to note about the English papers is that most of the exams are closed-book. This means that you cannot take the texts that you've been studying into the exam. So, you'll have to remember the plot of the text, as well as general themes and other content that you may be tested on. Of course, it is also important to remember specific quotations from the texts you have studied, in order to back up analysis you have made and show the marker your knowldge of the text.

English Literature

Assessment for English Literature focuses on four main areas. These four areas are split into two separate papers. These areas are:

- **Shakespeare** – Studying a Shakespeare play.

- **Post-1914 Literature** – Studying a British play or novel written after 1914.

- **19th Century Literature** – Studying a novel from the 19th century.

- **Poetry** – Studying and comparing poems from a poetry anthology, followed by a comparison of two unseen poems.

The first paper covers Shakespeare and post-1914 literature, whilst the second paper focuses on 19th century literature and poetry.

All of the questions in this exam are essay-based. So, you will be expected to write a longer piece of work, usually talking about the subject or themes of the text(s) that the question specifies. The questions that you should answer will vary depending on what texts you've read during lessons. Be sure to answer the questions on the books you've covered!

English Language

Like English Literature, English Language is separated into four main parts. These are:

*   **Reading Fiction** – Reading an unseen extract then answering questions about it.

*   **Imaginative Writing** – A creative writing task.

*   **Non-fictional Reading** – Answering questions on two unseen non-fiction extracts.

*   **Non-fictional Writing** – A non-fiction writing task.

Paper one contains questions on reading fiction and imaginative writing, whilst non-fictional reading and writing are reserved for the second paper.

Like English Literature, these questions are mostly essay-based. However, these essays will not be as long, since you will be asked multiple questions in a single section.

Tips for English Revision

Sadly, revising for English can be a bit of a pain. Outside

of practising your spelling, grammar and handwriting, the best way to get better at English essays is to write them. Preferably, you should try to write these under exam conditions, using the same timings as those in the real exam.

Learn the Material. The first step to success at English GCSE is to know what you're talking about. Make sure you read the books, plays or poems that you need to answer questions on the exam. If it helps, find film adaptations which are faithful to the original material – this can help you visualise the events of the novel or play more easily.

On top of this, there are plenty of websites and books which offer interpretations and critiques of the texts that you're studying. You can use these as a guide to the text, or as arguments in your essays.

For plays and novels, you should try to remember the key events which take place, as well as the main characters and their personalities. Creating a small fact file with profiles for each character can be a fun way of summarising them and their role in the text. If it helps, you can even use descriptions of the characters' looks to sketch them, giving you a broader picture of what they would be like.

For the story, try to reduce the book into the key events. Preferably, try to find the three key events of the text – the ones which define its three acts. Then, reduce these three chunks into three smaller events, meaning that you have nine events which drive the plot of the novel or play. You can then sort these events into a flowchart so that you can easily remember the order of events.

From here, the nine key events could be:

• Romeo and Juliet attend the ball

• Romeo and Juliet meet

• The balcony scene occurs

• Romeo meets with Friar Lawrence to make wedding arrangements

• Lord Capulet arranges for Juliet to marry Paris

• Romeo kills Tybalt and is banished

• Juliet takes the drug to feign her death

• Romeo drinks the poison upon finding Juliet 'dead' in her tomb

• Juliet awakens to find Romeo's body, then takes her own life

Finally, you will need to remember the core themes for the novel, play or poem. Generally, the texts you study will have one or two primary themes (in the case of *Romeo and Juliet*, these might be 'love' and 'fate'). In addition to this, there may be a few minor themes. Additional reading of secondary sources, such as literary criticism, will reveal some of these ideas. Experiment with different revision techniques which suit you in order to remember the key themes of the text, as well as key events, characters, or lines of the text which relate to them.

Sadly, English at GCSE often requires you to remember key quotes. This can be annoying, but the best way to learn them is to read them, write them or listen to them being spoken over and over until they stick in your head.

Answer Practice Questions. Once you're confident that you know all of the different characters, story events, and themes of your text, it's time to get to work on practice questions. As usual, get hold of some past papers and answer all of the questions that are relevant to your course.

If you get tired of writing whole essays, then at least you can attempt writing essay plans for them. This will still test your knowledge and ability to structure an answer, even if it doesn't completely match the experience of writing a full essay.

The most difficult part of using practice questions to revise for English is that you will need to find someone to read and mark your essay, so that you know where you're doing well, and where you need to improve. Ask your teacher if it's possible for them to take a look at your essays or essay plans, and they might be able to give you some pointers, giving you a rough idea of what to work on next.

Read the Mark Schemes. Unlike the mark schemes for Maths and Science, which contain right or wrong answers, the marking criteria for English exams is a bit more abstract. In an English exam, you aren't necessarily being marked on what your argument is, but rather how well you argue it, and how clear your message is. This is reflected in the mark scheme, where clarity in writing and how robust your argument is valued most. Take a look at the mark schemes for the exams that you're sitting to see exactly what is being asked of you.

Practise Spelling, Grammar, Punctuation and Handwriting. These are important when it comes to scoring high marks in English. A portion of the marks awarded in an exam are based on your grasp of spelling, grammar and punctuation, so it pays to practise those as much as possible. Practising these can be tricky, but the best way to get through it is to learn general rules. The way you communicate your points is what gains you the marks in GCSE English, and good communication requires good spelling, grammar and punctuation.

Handwriting is vital because the examiner needs to be able to read what you have written in order to mark it accurately. If the examiner can't read your work, they won't mark it. Therefore, you should spend some time practising handwriting if you think yours isn't up to standard. You'll probably be writing very quickly in the exam, which means that your handwriting will probably be less legible than usual. Doing practice essays is a good way to find ways of making your handwriting neater, especially if you do the mock exams under timed conditions. If it helps, cut out joined-up handwriting in favour of print handwriting, so that the examiner is more likely to be able to understand what words you've written.

In the exam…

Always have a plan. When it comes to success at English GCSE, the most valuable thing is to plan your essay before you begin. Once you open your exam paper, you might find a question that's perfect. You might be tempted to go head-first into your answer because you want to secure the marks, but it pays to exercise restraint and take the question more slowly. The length of the exam is designed to allow students to write a quick plan before starting each question, so you won't be losing time to spend on your essay if you take a moment to write a plan. In fact, planning will make your time much more valuable, since you'll have a good idea of what direction your answer is going in.

Planning your answer is beneficial for two reasons. Firstly, it'll force you to look at the question more closely. This means that you'll answer the actual question in the paper, rather than misinterpret it or create a question in your head that you would like to answer. Many students fail to answer the question directly, and planning will help you clarify what's being asked of you in the exam.

A plan will also help you stick to the point of the essay. As you write an answer, you can slowly drift away from the main point and get side-tracked by minor details which aren't entirely relevant to the question. Staying relevant is vital when doing your English exams. You don't have enough time to talk about everything surrounding a book, play, poem or other topic, so you need to focus on exactly what the question is asking. When you write your plan, you can list details which are strictly relevant, and cut out anything you don't need. For example, say you had the following question:

What is the significance of fate in Romeo and Juliet?

It may be tempting to discuss every major theme or event in *Romeo and Juliet*, but only a handful are relevant to the question. You plan may look something like this:

Introduction

- No need to explain the plot of the play – head straight into your answer.

- Quickly explain what is meant by fate – forces beyond the characters' control determine their lives and deaths.

Main Point 1

- "star-cross'd lovers".

- Romeo and Juliet are fated to meet one another, spend a brief period of time together, then be separated forever.

Main Point 2

- Romeo and Juliet both come from completely opposing families, yet still fall in love with one another.

- Their love appears to transcend (go beyond) their families. It could be argued that fate has caused that to occur.

Main Point 3

- The message sent to Romeo about Juliet feigning her death happens to arrive at the wrong time.

- Mercutio: "a plague on both your houses" foreshadows the death of both Romeo and Juliet.

- Forces outside of Romeo and Juliet's control seals their fate.

Conclusion

- Fate controls almost every aspect of *Romeo and Juliet*. Fates brings them together and fate tears them away from one another.

You plan doesn't even need to be this detailed – it's just a space to quickly jot down the main ideas for your essay, giving you a map of the direction you're taking your answer in. It's also helpful because it means you don't have to keep remembering key points – you'll have them written there for easy reference.

Once your plan is finished, draw a line through it to show the examiners marking your essay that it isn't your essay. Then you can get to work!

Make a point, provide evidence, then explain it. This is one of the best ways to structure your answers in an English exam, or any other test which is essay-based, and requires you to form an argument. However, this method won't work for the creative writing exercises.

1. Make your point – Here, you need to make a claim which relates to the question. For example, "One of

the main themes in *Romeo and Juliet* is fate."

2. Provide evidence – depending on what exam you are sitting, the type of evidence you provide might change. For an English exam, you're likely to take a quote from the text, for example, "A pair of star-cross'd lovers take their life." For other subjects, such as History or Geography, you might provide statistics instead of a quote.

3. Explain it – Finally, you need to link your evidence to the point that you've made. In this case, you might say "the phrase 'star-cross'd' implies that Romeo and Juliet were destined to meet each other for a brief moment in time, only to be pulled away from each other in death."

This method is excellent for structuring an argument, and can work throughout an essay. Remember to always link your argument to the question by saying something along the lines of "this relates to the question because…". This shows the examiner that you understand how what you are writing relates to the overall topic. For extra marks, you can show how your points link to one another as well, showing that you have a more complete picture of what you are writing about.

Science – Revision and Exam

So far, we've discussed two very different kinds of exam: Maths exams, which focus on right and wrong answers (and how you got to them); and English exams, which is more about longer pieces of writing, and how you communicate your ideas (rather than what your ideas are). Maths papers tend to be built up on multiple shorter questions, whilst an English exam is usually made up of only a handful of much longer essays.

GCSE Science takes a bit from both types of exam. On the one hand, science papers are a lot like maths ones – there are right and wrong answers. The questions come in a variety of sizes. Some will be one-word, one-mark answers, whilst others will require a longer piece of writing to gain full marks. So, it's like maths in that you can be right or wrong, but it's a bit more like English in that you will need to remember written ideas rather than simply mathematical techniques (although there are some maths-related questions as well).

Science at GCSE level is split into three different subjects: physics, biology and chemistry. You will sit separate papers for each of these subjects. Each of these subjects has two exams, which means that there are six science exams that you will have to take before you achieve your GCSE.

The exact topics of your course will differ depending on your exam board – you can find the content of each subject on the specification pages of their respective websites.

Your exam board also determines how long each exam is, and how valuable they are:

Science GCSE - From 2014 to 2017

	AQA	Edexcel
Physics paper 1	1 hour 60 marks Worth 25% of physics GCSE	1 hour 60 marks Worth 25% of physics GCSE
Physics paper 2	1 hour 60 marks Worth 25% of physics GCSE	1 hour 60 marks Worth 25% of physics GCSE
Physics paper 3	1 hour 60 marks Worth 25% of physics GCSE	1 hour 60 marks Worth 25% of physics GCSE
Physics controlled assessment	2 written assessments 50 marks Worth 25% of physics GCSE	One or more written assessments 50 marks Worth 25% of physics GCSE
Biology paper 1	1 hour 60 marks Worth 25% of biology GCSE	1 hour 60 marks Worth 25% of biology GCSE

Biology paper 2	1 hour 60 marks Worth 25% of biology GCSE	1 hour 60 marks Worth 25% of biology GCSE
Biology paper 3	1 hour 60 marks Worth 25% of biology GCSE	1 hour 60 marks Worth 25% of biology GCSE
Biology controlled assessment	2 written assessments 50 marks Worth 25% of biology GCSE	One or more written assessments 50 marks Worth 25% of biology GCSE
Chemistry paper 1	1 hour 60 marks Worth 25% of chemistry GCSE	1 hour 60 marks Worth 25% of chemistry GCSE
Chemistry paper 2	1 hour 60 marks Worth 25% of chemistry GCSE	1 hour 60 marks Worth 25% of chemistry GCSE

Chemistry paper 3	1 hour	1 hour
	60 marks	60 marks
	Worth 25% of chemistry GCSE	Worth 25% of chemistry GCSE
Chemistry controlled assessment	2 written assessments	One or more written assessments
	50 marks	50 marks
	Worth 25% of chemistry GCSE	Worth 25% of chemistry GCSE

Science GCSE - From 2018 Onwards

	AQA	Edexcel
Physics paper 1	1 hour, 45 minutes 100 marks Worth 50% of physics GCSE	1 hour, 10 minutes 60 marks Worth 16.67% of science GCSE
Physics paper 2	1 hour, 45 minutes 100 marks Worth 50% of physics GCSE	1 hour, 10 minutes 60 marks Worth 16.67% of science GCSE
Biology paper 1	1 hour, 45 minutes 100 marks Worth 50% of biology GCSE	1 hour, 10 minutes 60 marks Worth 16.67% of science GCSE
Biology paper 2	1 hour, 45 minutes 100 marks Worth 50% of biology GCSE	1 hour, 10 minutes 60 marks Worth 16.67% of science GCSE
Chemistry paper 1	1 hour, 45 minutes 100 marks Worth 50% of chemistry GCSE	1 hour, 10 minutes 60 marks Worth 16.67% of science GCSE

Chemistry paper 2	1 hour, 45 minutes	1 hour, 10 minutes
	100 marks	60 marks
	Worth 50% of chemistry GCSE	Worth 16.67% of science GCSE

Like with GCSE Maths, you can use this breakdown of time and marks to figure out how much time you should spend on each question.

Tips for Science Revision

As previously mentioned, you will need to learn a lot of facts for GCSE Science. You'll need to memorise diagrams of things like plants, atomic structure and the human body, as well as mathematical formulas for calculating changes in energy (for chemistry) and electricity (in physics). Of all the compulsory subjects, Science may be the most diverse in what is asked of you, since questions can involve completing images, performing mathematical operations, and simply recalling information.

The style of your answer can come in many different forms as well. Some questions will be multiple-choice, whilst others will be single, one-word answers. Towards the end of the exam, you'll likely come across longer questions which require extended pieces of writing, as well as longer mathematical questions. You need to prepare for these types of questions.

Learn the material. Learning material for the sciences is fairly straight forward, since it mostly boils down to right or wrong answers. Depending on what type of learner you are, there's a range of revision methods that work well for science at GCSE level.

If you're a kinaesthetic learner, flashcards can be a great way for matching the names of concepts to their definitions. For example, you could write the names of each part of a plant or animal cell on one side of the card, and then what they look like or their function on the other. GCSE Science often requires you to know concepts and their names, and often you'll need to be able to explain them in an answer, or apply them. So, flashcards are a great way to retain some of the most important information.

You're also in luck if you're a visual learner, since a lot of scientific processes and occurrences are portrayed with diagrams. You can have a go at committing these to memory by memorising the diagram, covering it up and then trying to draw it out for yourself. This can be useful for remembering all kinds of scientific processes.

Aural learners can make use of a wide range of podcasts and videos on GCSE Science content. See the useful resources section at the end of this book to get some ideas on where to start.

Brush up on your maths. As previously mentioned, you will need to do some mathematical problem solving in your science papers. Calculators are permitted, so you don't need to worry about working on your mental arithmetics, but you will need to remember one or two formulas in order to solve some of the questions. Depending on the subject, year, and exam board, some formulas may be written for you in the opening pages of the exam paper. Have a look at some papers from previous years and see what they give you, then focus on the formulas that you have to remember. There are mnemonics and diagrams which can help make the formulas easier to digest.

Attempt practice papers. As always, practice papers are the best way to get an idea of where you're comfortably scoring marks, and where you need to improve. It's recommended to try and take a paper in one sitting, under timed exam conditions. However, individual questions can be taken from past papers and attempted separately in order to test your knowledge on a specific topic.

For Science, the mark scheme is straightforward because the answers are either right or wrong, with little room for ambiguity. This means that you can mark your own paper once you've finished it, or have a friend or family member mark it for you.

In the exam…

Once the exam starts, write down any of the formulas or key concepts that you know will come up, either on a blank piece of paper or somewhere on your answer booklet (not in an answer box, and remember draw a line through it so the examiner doesn't mark it). This means that you can quickly refer to these notes rather than worrying about remembering them constantly.

Generally, Science exams are split into topics. This means that, for example, all of the questions on magnetism and electromagnetism will be grouped together in the physics paper. Quite often, the questions in a section will get more demanding as they progress, and then the difficulty 'curve' of questions will reset once the next section begins. So, you can (and should) start with whichever section you are most comfortable with, complete it, then move onto tougher areas.

Languages – Revision and Exam

Depending on your school, you may or may not have to take a Modern Foreign Language GCSE. Regardless, you may have chosen to study French, Spanish, German or another language at GCSE level. Whatever the case, you need to be as prepared for languages as you can be.

Whatever language GCSEs you happen to be taking, there are multiple aspects and revision techniques that are common throughout all of the different courses. Therefore, this section will discuss Language GCSEs in a general sense rather than discussing individual languages.

Language GCSEs are made up of four different exams: listening, speaking, reading and writing. The lengths and value of each of these exams will differ based on your exam board, but there tends to be approximately equal weight for each exam. This means that each exam is worth around 25% of your overall GCSE.

Here is a breakdown of the four exams:

Listening

This exercise is used to test your ability to understand the language you are studying in its spoken form. Students need to listen to an extract which is played, and write down answers based on the material being read. The extract will be spoken in the language you are studying (e.g. French or Spanish). In the first section, the questions are written in English and must be answered in the language you are studying, whilst the second section contains questions written in the foreign language, which must be answered in English. You are given some time to read the questions before the listening exercise begins.

Speaking

This assessment is used to evaluate your speaking skills in the language you're studying. Exercises include role-plays, photo cards and free conversation. Generally, speaking assessments in languages are taken a few weeks before the exam period begins.

Reading

This exam tests your ability to read a piece of writing in the language you're studying, then answer questions based on it. In section A, the questions will be written in English, and you must answer them in the language you've studied. Section B is the opposite: questions are written in the language that you've studied, and must be answered in English. The final section tests your translation skills; you will be presented with several words which you must translate from the language you've studied into English. Depending on your exam board, and whether you're taking a foundation-tier exam or higher-tier exam, the number of words you must translate will differ.

Writing

The focus of the writing exam is to assess your ability to communicate ideas in the language you've been studying. This involves translation, structured writing tasks and open-ended writing tasks. The exact structure of the exam depends on whether you are sitting foundation or higher-tier. Further details can be found on your exam board's website, under the specification section.

Tips for Languages Revision

As you can see from the above breakdown, Language GCSEs utilise multiple kinds of question and format to test you. You'll have to speak, write, read and listen in the language that you're studying, and preparing for all of these can be quite difficult. This section will split revision tips into these four categories, although you may find that some of them cross over into one another:

Listening

Spend time listening to the language you're studying. This may seem obvious, but many students don't know where to start when it comes to finding material to listen to. Listening to music in the language that you're studying can be helpful, as you'll become accustomed with the speed and tone of the language, as well as be introduced to a considerable vocabulary – all in easily digestible songs. Films and television are also a safe bet, particularly when they were written and filmed in the language (rather than dubbed in it). You can watch these with English subtitles if it helps – it will give you an insight into how the language is spoken. It doesn't replace revision, but it acts as a great supplement to your studies and can be used as a break from long periods of note-taking.

Learn your vocabulary. A strong vocabulary is incredibly valuable for both listening and reading exams, since you'll need to figure out what words are written or being spoken. 'Vocab lists' are a great way of memorising the words you'll need to know. During your course, you'll be introduced to words associated with certain topics, such as culture and politics. Words revolving around these areas will be likely to show up in your exam, so you should take the time to learn those subjects. Vocab lists will likely be available in your textbooks, as well as appearing in online resources. You can use them by looking at the word, covering up its meaning in English, then writing down what you think it means. Once you can do that easily, do it the other way around – look at the word in English, then write it in the language that you're studying. If possible, use online resources to listen to how the words sound as well. Audio vocabulary lists can be used by listening to a word, then writing down the English translation.

Don't forget about tenses. There are lots of different

tenses and verb forms in French and Spanish, and they are vital for getting marks in almost every assessment in languages. Tenses are important in listening tests because you might be asked "true or false" questions that focus on your knowledge of them. For example, the exercise might say "Mark plays football in his spare time" (in the foreign language). You can then be asked the question:

"Mark used to play football regularly." True or False?

If you didn't know your tenses, a question like this could completely catch you out, since the statement in the question says that Mark *used* to play football, which is a different tense to "Mark plays football", the phrase in the listening exercise. Questions like this can show up in the listening exercise, so it's important you take the time to learn them. Online quizzes and games can test your ability to spot which tenses are appropriate for a sentence, and in turn this will help you recognise the tenses as they show up in the exam.

Speaking

Preparing for the speaking assessment is very different to studying for other exams. Unlike almost every other exam you'll take at GCSE, you aren't assessed on written work in the speaking assessment, but rather your ability to communicate ideas clearly by speaking in a foreign language.

Speaking tests take place earlier than other exams. You'll probably sit your speaking assessment a few weeks earlier than you sit the rest of your exams. This can be a problem for people who don't take this into account, but if you know what you're doing, you can benefit from having this come earlier. Make sure your revision for the speaking test takes place earlier in the revision period, so you have as much time to study for it as possible.

Listen to how people speak. By no means are you expected to have a perfect accent, but knowing how words are pronounced is necessary for making sure you can communicate effectively during the speaking test. Listening to music and finding audio examples of conversation in the language online will give you an idea of what tone people use when speaking, and how the words are pronounced.

Make use of your supervised preparation time. The notes you make in this period are permitted in the assessment, so make sure that they're helpful. Keep the notes concise and have prepared phrases ready – particularly ones which make good use of tenses and verbs – to show off your knowledge.

Be appropriate. The speaking test focuses on appropriate use of vocabulary and grammar, so make sure you stick to the point and don't go overboard. Waffle or filling space to make your answers and conversation seem more sophisticated than they are won't work – try to be direct as possible with your answers.

Reading

Practise your reading. This section essentially tests your comprehension skills in the language that you've studied. You'll have to answer questions based on the text, demonstrating your understanding of the language. So, that means you need to be proficient in reading text in this language.

One of the best ways to improve your understanding is to extend your vocabulary, so you're less likely to come across words that you don't understand. Depending on your course, your exam board may release a full vocabulary list, containing all of the words you need to know the meaning of in order to secure a good grade in the assessment. If this is made available to you, make full use of it to construct flashcards, write notes, or record yourself speaking the word in English as well as the language you've studied. Even if an official vocabulary list isn't provided by the exam board, textbooks, workbooks and online resources are available which can be used as a checklist to make sure you know every word necessary.

On top of this, it might be useful to read books, articles and other materials in the language that you're studying. This is particularly helpful if you find things to read which share the topics that your exam will cover. Online resources are great for this since foreign-language news articles can often be accessed easily and for free. You might learn some interesting things about the countries which speak the language, too!

Grammar is still important. In some ways, you can

think of the reading test as a written version of the listening test – although they will likely contain different content. In both, you are given some material to consume (either by reading or listening), and then you will need to answer questions on them. Earlier in this chapter, we mentioned that the listening test requires a strong grasp on grammar and tenses in order to answer the questions effectively. The same is the case here in the reading exam. The text could read "Mark plays football regularly." If you don't know your tenses, you could get caught out by the following question:

"Mark used to play football regularly." True or False?

The answer is false, because Mark still plays football regularly, according to the text. However, getting your tenses mixed up could result in you not answering questions properly. Make sure to brush up on grammar and tenses before this exam.

Writing

For the writing exam, you will need to be able to communicate ideas in a written format. This means you'll need to utilise a number of different skills, and have quite a vast pool of knowledge at the ready. All of the above sections on grammar and vocabulary apply here.

Get hold of some practice papers. Past papers and sample questions are going to be useful for several reasons. Firstly, you can use them to practise writing responses to the questions. If possible, give them to your teacher to mark.

The other reason why practice papers are so useful for this exam is that there's a range of different types of question, and you need to prepare yourself for them. There are open-ended writing tasks, closed writing tasks and translation exercises, amongst other activities in the writing exam. With such a large variety, you need to familiarise yourself with what these types of question look like, and what's expected of you.

In the exam…

As previously mentioned, GCSE Languages exams are varied in their content, format and focus. For this reason, not every piece of advice for one kind of exam will suit the others very well.

For the reading and writing tests, make sure you answer the questions that you find easiest first. There might be a question on a topic you remember more vocabulary for, so you should head straight into that first before you forget anything.

For every assessment except the speaking test, make sure you write some key words, phrases or grammar rules on your answer paper as soon as the exam begins. This means you can refer to them at any time. However, remember to draw a line through these notes before the exam finishes, so that the examiner knows not to mark it.

History – Revision and Exam

History at GCSE level is incredibly broad, covering a

range of different topics. In this section, you'll get tips which apply to whatever periods of time that you're studying. Students finishing their History GCSE in 2017 will also have a piece of coursework to complete. This is usually worth around 25% of your GCSE, but may differ depending on your exam board and course. Students who have started their GCSEs in 2016 or later will not need to do coursework since this has been removed from the curriculum.

Topics studied for History GCSE span from Tudor England and the history of medicine, to Nazi Germany, Soviet Russia and the American West. Generally, students study four different topics, each covering a different overall theme. You'll be tested on knowledge primarily, but you'll also need to examine and assess sources such as images and pieces of unseen text.

History exams are made up of lots of smaller essays. Think of these as essays in format (i.e. a longer written piece rather than a single-word or single-sentence answer) but shorter than those found in an English GCSE paper. There will be multiple mini-essays for each period or area of history that you've studied. Unlike some other exams in other subjects, you will not get to choose which questions you answer.

Tips for History Revision

Revising for History is similar to revising for other essay-based subjects such as English. You are being tested on your knowledge, but also on presenting that knowledge accurately and clearly to the examiner.

Get your facts straight. Knowing facts is vitally important for doing well at History GCSE. In some questions, you may be asked to analyse or evaluate events and concepts, but in order to do this you need to have a strong foundation of knowledge. For example, you can't evaluate the impact of the Munich Putsch on the rise of the Nazis without knowing what the Munich Putsch was, or who the Nazi party were. So, the first thing you should do is gather your notes and learn the facts.

There are a few things to note when heading into revision. First, it's important that you know when things happened. You don't need to know the exact date for every event that happened, but at least have the key dates down. More importantly, you need to have a timeline of events. This is important because knowing the order which events played out means you can analyse the cause and effect in history. Constructing timelines and memorising them is a great way for visual learners to remember the order of events, whilst audio learners could record themselves reading out the events in order, and then play it back to themselves. If you are a kinaesthetic learner, you can make use of activities such as timelines with only some events filled in – leaving you to complete it.

As always, flashcards are a great way to revise the details of events. On one side of the card, write the name of the event or concept, then on the other write down its meaning, or what happened. You can then match your flashcard up to your timeline if it helps.

Finally, fact files can be a useful way of remembering the key players in history. Take note of their name, their profession or job, as well as their role in historical events. In some cases, it may also be helpful to take note of their background. This will help you get a more complete picture of the time periods that you are studying.

Look at sources. Sources will be the focus of some of the questions you need to answer in your History exams. For these, you'll need to look at a source – either a piece of text or an image – and discuss it. You'll be required to talk about its message, historical significance, who it might be aimed at and the person (or people) who created it. You won't know exactly what sources you will be asked about in the exam, so you just need to gather general knowledge of your topics and be ready to employ any of it. However, you can look at sources in your textbook or past papers for practice.

Make use of practice papers. Practice papers are great because the questions are full of lots of medium-length questions. This means you can take just a few questions from a paper if you want to focus on a specific topic, or sit the whole thing under exam conditions. This will help you get your timings down, which is important for the history exams.

Read the mark scheme. History is somewhat like Maths in that you are dealing with facts, but a bit more like English because you need to discuss them, analyse them and in some cases form arguments. By reading the mark scheme, you get an idea of what types of things examiners are looking for. Generally, they want you to be able to display your knowledge and understanding, but they also want you to show this in a clear way. By reading the mark scheme, you'll get an idea of what hoops you need to jump through in order to secure the marks.

In the exam…

Stick to the point. Use the "point, evidence, explain" method described in the English section of this chapter to make sure you stay to the point for every question. Since the exams are made up of lots of smaller questions, it isn't appropriate to write plans – it isn't worth it. Instead, make sure you link your statements back to the question somehow. Whenever you're about to make a point, think "how does this relate to the question?" Make sure you have a clear idea of how all your points are relevant before writing.

Keep an eye on the time. Timing is key in every exam, but History has lots of medium-length questions which can be hard to hit a sweet-spot in terms of time spent per question. As always, figure out how much time to approximately spend on each question by looking at how many marks are available.

Go for the easiest questions first. In some cases, the questions will be part of a larger, connected section, where you're best off starting with the first question. However, you can look through all of the questions and pick which is best for you.

Geography – Revision and Exam

Like GCSE History, the Geography curriculum is in the process of changing. If you are finishing your GCSEs in 2017, then you will have to do (or have already done) a fieldwork assignment conducted as controlled assessment. Depending on your exam board, this will be worth around 25% of your GCSE course.

If you started your GCSEs in 2016 and you're sitting your exams in 2018 or later, this fieldwork will be combined with an exam. Depending on your exam board, the details of this will change. Some exam boards involve you creating completing a fieldwork booklet around 3 months before your exam. This booklet is then taken into one of your 3 exams and is used as a resource for answering questions.

Regardless of whether you are sitting your Geography GCSE in 2017, 2018 or later, you must sit 3 exams. Each of these covers different topics, including human and natural geography.

Tips for Geography Revision

Learn key terms. From 'abrasion' to 'zero population growth', there's a wealth of terms that you must know in order to perform well in GCSE Geography. Like History, you might be asked to write more critical pieces of work in your exam, but this analysis needs a foundational knowledge in all kinds of key terms. Thankfully, there are plenty of resources online which contain full lists of the jargon you'll need to know, along with definitions and examples. Make flashcards out of these if you find it useful, or maybe try your hand at a quiz where you need to match up the terms to their definitions. Either way, make sure you know what the term is called as well as what it means.

Complete your coursework to the best of your ability. This might sound obvious, but plenty of students neglect their coursework because they think they can just make up the marks in their exam, or the lack of strict time constraints doesn't motivate them to complete their controlled assessments adequately. Think of it this way: the better you perform in your coursework, the more marks you'll have going into the exam. Coursework is an excellent opportunity to bank marks and have them secured. So, if anything does happen to go wrong in the exam – say you're unlucky with the questions given, or you blank on key information – it isn't the end of the world because you'll have already scored some points in the coursework.

In the case of students sitting their exams in 2018 or later, this isn't quite the same. You aren't being marked directly on your coursework, but rather you're using your coursework as a resource in the exam. Still, completing your resource booklet well means that you'll be better prepared for the exam.

In the exam...

Depending on the year you sit the paper, and what exam board you are on, the exact content of your paper and its structure will differ. However, you can expect the following kinds of question in all of your Geography exams:

- Multiple-choice;

- Short, one-word or one-sentence;

- Levels of response – a question that can grant more marks depending on what kind of answer you give;

- Extended prose – longer, essay-style questions.

<u>Regardless of what exam you're sitting, here are some tips which you should bear in mind while sitting the exam.</u>

Geography is about facts, but also analysis. Facts are important, but sometimes you need to employ more critical or analytic methods when answering questions. If the question asks you to 'discuss' a point, or offers a quote that you need to provide evidence for, you need to be thinking about *why* something is the case, not just what is the case. In these types of question, just rattling off facts isn't enough – you need to go a little further and be more analytic. Don't try and get too ambitious in your answer (you're not writing a thesis!) but you do need to consider beyond the simple task of description.

Read and analyse images and figures carefully. Many questions in your Geography exams will require you to examine a source of some kind, and answer questions based on it. These can include photographs, satellite imagery, maps and graphs. Make sure you're ready to answer questions of this kind before going into the exam, and always read them carefully before starting to answer the associated questions. There's nothing worse than answering a whole section of questions only to realise you've misinterpreted the sources given to you.

Conclusion

Summary

So, you now know all the tips we can give you for acing your GCSEs. You've learnt what GCSEs are, how they're marked and graded, and why they matter. You've also been introduced to a number of revision techniques, and hopefully had the opportunity to find out what type of learner you are. In addition, you've been given the rundown on exams and coursework, and you know how to combat stress. Finally, we've provided some subject-specific advice so that you can focus your studies and get the best marks possible.

One thing to take away from this book is that GCSEs aren't the most important thing in the world. They might feel like that while you're studying for them, with what feels like a mountain to overcome, but once they're over and you get your results, you should feel satisfied (and proud) of what you've accomplished. Make use of the tips we've provided in this book, try your best, and go away from your GCSEs knowing that you've done something impressive and commendable.

A Few Final Words…

You have reached the end of your guide to passing your GCSEs with level 9s. If you have read the information in this book and made use of the tips provided, you should be on your way to passing your GCSEs comfortably and making yourself proud. Hopefully, you will feel far more confident in what you know as well as what you need to improve.

For any test, it is helpful to consider the following in mind...

The Three P's

1. **Preparation.** Preparation is key to passing any test; you won't be doing yourself any favours by not taking the time to prepare. Many fail their tests because they did not know what to expect or did not know what their own weaknesses were. Take the time to re-read any areas you may have struggled with. By doing this, you will become familiar with how you will perform on the day of the test.

2. **Perseverance.** If you set your sights on a goal and stick to it, you are more likely to succeed. Obstacles and setbacks are common when trying to achieve something great, and you shouldn't shy away from them. Instead, face the tougher parts of the test, even if you feel defeated. If you need to, take a break from your work to relax and then return with renewed vigour. If you fail the test, take the time to consider why you failed, gather your strength and try again.

3. **Performance.** How well you perform will be the result of your preparation and perseverance. Remember to relax when taking the test and try not to panic. Believe in your own abilities, practice as much as you can, and motivate yourself constantly. Nothing is gained without hard work and determination, and this applies to how you perform on the day of the test.

Good luck with your GCSEs. We wish you the best of luck in all of your future endeavours!

Useful
Resources

	Monday	Tuesday	Wednesday	Thursday	Friday	Saturday	Sunday
9:00am-10:00am							
10:00am-11:00am							
11:00am-12:00am							
12:00am-01:00pm							
01:00pm-02:00pm							
02:00pm-03:00pm							

03:00pm–04:00pm	04:00pm–05:00pm	05:00pm–06:00pm	06:00pm–07:00pm	07:00pm–08:00pm

	Monday	Tuesday	Wednesday	Thursday	Friday	Saturday	Sunday
9:00am-10:00am							
10:00am-11:00am							
11:00am-12:00am							
12:00am-01:00pm							
01:00pm-02:00pm							
02:00pm-03:00pm							

03:00pm- 04:00pm							
04:00pm- 05:00pm							
05:00pm- 06:00pm							
06:00pm- 07:00pm							
07:00pm- 08:00pm							

	Monday	Tuesday	Wednesday	Thursday	Friday	Saturday	Sunday
9:00am-10:00am							
10:00am-11:00am							
11:00am-12:00am							
12:00am-01:00pm							
01:00pm-02:00pm							
02:00pm-03:00pm							

03:00pm-04:00pm						
04:00pm-05:00pm						
05:00pm-06:00pm						
06:00pm-07:00pm						
07:00pm-08:00pm						

	Monday	Tuesday	Wednesday	Thursday	Friday	Saturday	Sunday
9:00am-10:00am							
10:00am-11:00am							
11:00am-12:00am							
12:00am-01:00pm							
01:00pm-02:00pm							
02:00pm-03:00pm							

03:00pm-04:00pm				
04:00pm-05:00pm				
05:00pm-06:00pm				
06:00pm-07:00pm				
07:00pm-08:00pm				

WANT FURTHER GUIDANCE FOR YOUR GCSEs?

CHECK OUT OUR OTHER GCSE GUIDES:

How2Become have created other FANTASTIC guides to help you prepare for a range of subjects at GCSE level:

FOR MORE INFORMATION ON OUR GCSE GUIDES, PLEASE CHECK OUT THE FOLLOWING:

WWW.HOW2BECOME.COM

NEED TO TAKE YOUR REVISION SKILLS TO THE NEXT LEVEL?

CHECK OUT OUR OTHER REVISION GUIDES:

FOR MORE INFORMATION ON OUR REVISION GUIDES, PLEASE CHECK OUT THE FOLLOWING:

WWW.HOW2BECOME.COM

Get Access To
FREE
GCSE Tests

www.MyEducationalTests.co.uk